THE SANIBEL SHELL GUIDE

BY
Margaret H. Greenberg

Cartoons by Roberta White Martin
Photographs and cover art by Nancy J. Olds

Anna Publishing, Inc.,

To Jacy From Nancy who it was great to have you here

Library of Congress
Catalog Card Number: 82-71090

International Standard Book Number: 0-89305-041-5

Printed in the U.S.A.

TABLE OF CONTENTS

FOREWORD

"It's mine! I saw it first!"

This book was written by an amateur sheller for other amateur shellers who would like to know something about the specimens they find on Sanibel and Captiva. You do not have to fly to the Philippines or the West Indies to find any shell in this guide. (You may, however, want to sneak off to a local shell shop if you absolutely must have a rare Lion's Paw for your collection.)

Many people do not realize that about seventy-five percent of the world's thousands of specimens are miniatures — that is, shells that are microscopic or no more than half an inch at maturity. Experts estimate that some 400 identified species can be found on Sanibel Island, but roughly three quarters of these specimens will be miniatures.

As a rule, amateur shellers do not crawl along the beach clutching a magnifying glass, or count the number of axial ribs in a particular specimen with the aid of a microscope. I have, of course, included a number of the more common (and visible) miniatures that you are likely to find. In keeping with my status as an amateur sheller, however, I have not attempted to poach on the territory of dedicated experts.

Over 100 shells (and other specimens) have been identified with the aid of photographs, sketches, and descriptions free of Latin words and technical jargon. You can find them all on Sanibel and Captiva.

There is a special chapter on when and where to shell on these Islands, information that is very rarely included in shell guides. There are also chapters on useful equipment for shellers, cleaning techniques, and simple shell craft. Finally, a map and an Index have been included for convenient reference.

I hope that you will find *The Sanibel Shell Guide* both informative and entertaining. Good luck with your shelling, and may you find a perfect Junonia!

Margaret H. Greenberg
Sanibel Island

CHAPTER 1

A FEW WORDS ABOUT SHELLS

𝕾𝖆𝖓𝖎𝖇𝖊𝖑 𝕲𝖔𝖙𝖍𝖎𝖈

A SHELLER'S PARADISE

Sanibel has often been called the "shell capital of the world." However, residents of the Sulu Islands, and those who live near a particular beach in Africa, claim precisely the same distinction for their fine shelling beaches. Therefore, it may be more prudent to say that Sanibel Island is the best shelling area in the United States, and the best within several thousand miles of our continental shores. Certainly no one will dispute the fact that Sanibel is a shell collector's paradise.

7

The question arises as to why Sanibel is blessed with such an enormous variety of lovely shells, so many of which are washed ashore intact. One explanation for this phenomenon lies in the fact that the Gulf of Mexico sends shells rolling across miles of sandy bottom towards our beaches. Even very fragile specimens stand a good chance of being washed ashore undamaged.

Off the shores of the Hawaiian Islands, for example, there are magnificent shells that rival anything found on Sanibel. However, these specimens rarely arrive on the beaches in one piece. The "Pacific" Ocean pounds them mercilessly against coral reefs, leaving only broken bits to wash ashore.

Of course, many other Barrier Islands also benefit from miles of sandy bottom offshore, largely devoid of such obstacles as rocks and coral reefs. Thus, one can find beautiful shells in many areas along Florida's west coast and Barrier Islands. However, Sanibel is different from all the other Barrier Islands in one important respect: its geographical position. Herein lies the true key to the mystery.

While other Barrier Islands have a north-south orientation, Sanibel's general orientation is east to west. The theory is that the Island's peculiar position in the Gulf of Mexico causes it to be, in effect, an enormous net, approximately 12 miles long. As a result, some rather rare specimens may wash up on our Gulf beaches after a good storm, along with other treasures. The highly-prized Junonia and the coveted Lion's Paw are good examples of rare shells that occasionally land on Sanibel. Neither shell is really "native" to the Island at all. When these mollusks are alive, they inhabit deep regions many miles beyond our shores.

MOLLUSKS AND THEIR SHELLS

A shell is actually the outer skeleton of an animal phylum called mollusks. Clams, oysters, snails, and mussels, for example, are all members of this phylum. Since a mollusk has no backbone, the animal protects himself by taking lime from the water and forming a calcium-based secretion to cover his soft, vulnerable body. Each thin layer of this secretion hardens immediately and, gradually, the shell is formed.

UNIVALVES AND BIVALVES

Mollusks are divided into two groups: univalves and bivalves. Univalves have one shell, generally spiral in shape. The animal, normally a snail, is curled up inside and firmly attached near the top of the shell by an extremely strong muscle. The foot, which propels the animal, is quickly drawn into the shell when the creature is threatened, and he quickly closes his door (operculum). Univalve snails are generally carnivorous, and very aggressively so. They feast on other shellfish by drilling holes in them, smothering them in a deadly embrace, injecting poison, or just prying them open.

Bivalves are two shells that are hinged together. Strong muscles attach the animal to the hinge on both sides. The feeding habits of bivalves are really quite civilized. They are equipped with a kind of strainer around the outer edges of the two shells. They take in water through this strainer, feed on the minute plants and marine animals, and then flush the water out.

MEASURING SHELLS

All the measurements in this book refer to the average size of mature specimens. You may well find shells that are larger, or smaller, than the average for a particular species.

The following diagrams indicate how one should measure different kinds of shells.

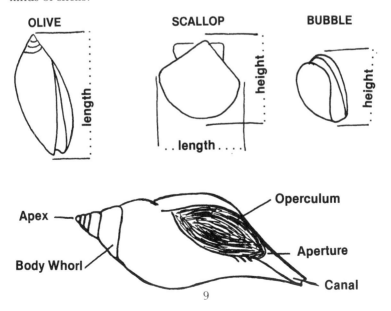

DESCRIBING SHELLS

One reason why people like to collect shells is the fact that their variety of color and marking seems to be almost infinite. One could, for example, spend an entire day gathering scallops on the beach — and no two specimens would be identical!

While the sheller may rejoice in the endless variety, anyone who attempts to describe various species is quickly frustrated, and most certainly in trouble. In this book, we have tried to describe shells in terms of the colors and markings that you are most likely to find on our Islands.

In describing shells, one invariably has to resort to words like "usually," "often," "commonly," "normally," "generally," etc. The highly-regrettable suffix "ish," when added to a word denoting color, covers a fairly broad spectrum. "Brownish" is not just plain brown. As long as the color of the shell suggests brown, "brownish" is a fairly safe and relatively accurate description

All books, including this one, will state that particular shells are spiny, thorny, or prickly. Since these words are often part of a shell's name (even in Latin), one cannot avoid using them. Therefore, beach shellers should realize that shells washed ashore are rarely in their original state. Spines, prickles, and thorns are bound to suffer from the ravages of a long ocean voyage.

With very few exceptions (we bought a Sundial and one valve of a Lion's Paw), the photographs in this book depict shells that were washed up on our beaches. We hope that pictures of typical beach specimens will help amateur shellers to identify what they have found. May you find more perfect specimens!

RESTRICTION ON GATHERING LIVE SHELLS

If you must have a live shell for your collection, you will want to observe Sanibel's live-shelling restriction: ONLY TWO LIVE SPECIMENS PER SPECIES PER PERSON.

In the interests of conservation, it is helpful to know that the live shells cast upon our shores by storms do not usually live to reproduce. However, specimens that you find living quite peacefully at low tide stand a very good chance of reproducing. The observance of Sanibel's live-shelling restriction will help to preserve a fine natural resource for the enjoyment of future generations.

CHAPTER 2

WHEN AND WHERE TO SHELL

"Beautiful shells roll right up to your feet!"

This is probably one of the most important chapters in our **Guide**. Many books will identify specimens that you have found, but none will tell you specifically where to look for good shells. Knowing where to shell is especially important for those who visit the Islands during the off-season months. When accommodations are less expensive, good shells are far less prevalent. However, there is no reason for you to go home without some fine specimens for your collection, no matter what time of year you visit Sanibel and Captiva.

LIVE-SHELLING RESTRICTION

Mellifluous phrases in slick brochures and ads lead many visitors to believe that Sanibel is still an unspoiled, undiscovered, tropical paradise where magnificent shells roll right up to their feet. This may all have been true — during the time of the Caloosa Indians.

In any event, Sanibel has certainly been discovered, and our once-plentiful supply of shells seems to be dwindling. In an effort to protect one of the Island's natural assets, the City of Sanibel has enacted a sensible restriction on live shelling: ONLY TWO LIVE SPECIMENS PER SPECIES PER PERSON.

There are still plenty of beautiful shells here; one just has to look a little harder to find them.

WHEN TO SHELL: BEST TIME OF YEAR, BEST TIME OF DAY

The most ideal combination of conditions for shelling would be the following: an exceptionally low morning tide during a full moon, a northwest wind, two or three days after a rousing storm during the high season. Since all these optimum conditions are not likely to occur at the same time, most shellers are happy to settle for any one of them.

There is no avoiding the fact that both the supply and the variety of shells are the greatest during the high-season months. This situation may help to console those who pay the highest possible hotel rates during the winter! A fine storm at any time of the year, or a northwest wind, help to stir up the shells. Those who visit during the summer months, when good shells are hard to find, can always pray for a rousing storm — but not a hurricane.

The best time of the day for shelling is entirely dependent upon the tides. Low tide is always the best time, for the receding waters expose sand bars and thousands of shells that are not at all visible when the tide is in. The low tides that occur during a full moon are often exceptionally low. You will certainly want to have a local tide chart, and you can pick ones up (free) at many hotels, marinas, and real estate offices.

WHERE TO SHELL: THE GULF SIDE

Many fine shellers are addicted to the Gulf side of the Islands, and certainly every kind of shell has been found here. Shells that were once way out in the Gulf, especially those that are not really native to the Islands, are much more likely to land on Gulf beaches.

Since so many resort accommodations are located right on the Gulf, all you have to do is go out the door and start shelling. Should you tire of a particular beach, or should you not be located on one, there are miles of other beaches to explore.

A word of caution. Sanibel recently enacted parking restrictions on some of its public beaches. (Restricted parking means parking by City permit only.) This decision prompted a storm of controversy, and restrictions were lifted in some areas. Observe any parking restriction signs that you may see: finding a Junonia may not be worth the hefty fine for violating them.

The following is a list of Gulf beaches where we have found many fine specimens. Consult the map for directions. All current parking restrictions (if any) and rest room facilities (if any) are indicated. If you want to try a particular beach that has parking restrictions, you may still be able to go there on a bicycle.

Lighthouse Point (Public Beach Access, No Parking Restrictions, Rest Room)
There is ample, shaded parking at this public beach access. You can see the exterior of the old lighthouse, and there is a permanent, outdoor shell exhibit nearby. Many short paths lead to the beach. Starfish are often abundant here.

End of Fulger Street (Public Beach Access, Restricted Parking)
The stretch of beach from the Ramada Inn to the Casa Ybel Resort, roughly two miles, is especially good for shelling. We have often had particularly good luck in the area between the posh Gulfside Place condominium complex and the Casa Ybel Resort.

End of Tarpon Bay Road (Public Beach Access, No Parking Restrictions)
This is a fine beach for shelling, and many visitors enjoy spending an entire day here. Should the parking places right at the beach be taken, there is ample free parking available just off Tarpon Bay Road.

Bowman's Beach (Public Beach Access, No Parking Restrictions)
In addition to being a fine shelling area, Bowman's Beach 'enjoys' a certain notoriety. Our local newspapers occasionally report the sighting of ''skinny dippers.'' Many shellers have found Sand Dollars on the sand bar off this beach, when the tide is very low.

Turner's Beach at Blind Pass (Public Beach Access, No Parking Restrictions, Rest Room)

This is an especially fine beach where many people like to spend an entire day. There are only two public-access beaches on Captiva. Although Turner's Beach has more parking spaces than the other one, it is always a good idea to arrive promptly.

Blind Pass used to be open, but a great storm filled it in a few years ago. Perhaps another storm will open it up again.

If you like to collect many kinds of scallop shells, this is definitely the beach to explore. One young child was so excited by the varieties of colorful scallop shells that she called this beach "a shell paradise."

Many people also enjoy long walks on either the Sanibel or the Captiva side of Blind Pass. Erosion has caused many trees to topple over onto the beach in a most dramatic fashion, and large pieces of driftwood make sunsets here a photographer's dream.

End of Sanibel-Captiva Road (Public Beach Access, No Parking Restrictions)

The second, and last, public beach access on Captiva is located near the end of the Island. There are very few parking spaces here, so you really must go early. You can walk (a few miles) all the way to Redfish Pass at the very tip of Captiva. Do not be tempted to swim across this pass to North Captiva. The current is exceedingly strong, and Redfish Pass is said to be a shortcut for sharks!

If you are looking for very large Quahog shells, this stretch of beach is a good place to find them. Of course, you are quite likely to find many other shells as well. In fact, this area may now have some very pleasant surprises for shellers. The reason for this phenomenon can be summed up in two words: the dredge.

By 1980, erosion in this area had become so severe that South Seas Plantation and many lovely (and very expensive) homes faced a dire threat. One could barely walk along parts of the beach, except at low tide, and high tides brought the sea perilously close to many residences. Thus a vast beach renourishment project was undertaken, at considerable expense. For many months, an off-shore dredge spewed forth countless tons of sand through large pipes and added many yards of beach to the endangered shoreline. This project was completed in the fall of 1981. The beach that you walk on today was probably under the water a short time ago.

Sand was not the only thing that came out of those pipes 24 hours a day for several months. Perfect specimens of all kinds of shells also landed on several miles of beach. Many eager shellers simply stood near the mouth of the pipe to grab what they could. The pipes and the dredge are no longer there, of course. But, for a long time to come, the tides will continue to bring in shells that were dislodged by the ambitious beach renourishment project.

WHERE TO SHELL: THE BAY SIDE
(San Carlos Bay and Pine Island Sound)

Many people do not think of shelling on the Bay side of Sanibel, i.e., San Carlos Bay and Pine Island Sound. There are several reasons for the relative lack of shelling on the Bay side. Approximately one third of Sanibel is a Federal Wildlife Sanctuary that affords no beach access, and this is almost entirely on the Bay side. Moreover, most accommodations are on, or near, the Gulf side. Finally, people tend to pass up the Bay side during the high season, when shells are quite plentiful on the Gulf beaches.

However, we have found that the Bay side of the Islands has some real treasures for shellers at any time of the year. During the summer months, a really dead time of the year for Gulf shelling, we have found large Horse Conchs, Whelks, and Kings' Crowns merely by wading in the Bay. Beautiful Sunray Venus clams lie exposed in the flats at low tide. If you enjoy feasting on crabs, there are always hundreds of them in the Bay, preparing to do battle as you wade by. We have also found an abundance of Sea Urchins and all kinds of clams and other shells during the off-season months.

Thus, if you visit our Islands during the off-season months, you can find excellent specimens on the Bay side at a time when the Gulf side is very disappointing indeed for shellers. You can always rent a small boat, of course, and explore the little islands and shores of Pine Island Sound and San Carlos Bay. However, you can also spare yourself that expense.

Lighthouse Point (Public Beach Access, No Parking Restrictions, Rest Room, See previous description under Gulf beaches)
You will come upon the public fishing pier soon after you round Lighthouse Point. You can walk and shell a long way from the Point towards the Causeway, until you reach a canal.

Beach Before Causeway (Public Beach Access, No Parking
  Restrictions)
  There is ample public parking at this beach access. It's a nice spot for
swimming and a bit of shelling.

The Causeway Road (Public Beach Access, No Parking Restrictions,
  Rest Rooms)
  Many people fish and picnic around the little islands on the Causeway
Road, but few people shell here. A family shelling trip to the Causeway
Road involves no toll. Parking is not restricted, and the second little
island after Sanibel has public rest rooms. There are trees for shade, picnic tables, even grills. In terms of shelling, we have had good luck on the
left side—as one drives off the Island. This is a good place to look for
various Tellin clams and Kings' Crowns. Sunsets here are often magnificent.

End of Bailey Road (Public Beach Access, Restricted Parking)
  Parking is by permit only at this beach, so you may have to go by bike.
You can see the remains of the old ferry dock and the original Bailey's
store. Shelling is good at low tide.

End of Dixie Beach Boulevard (Public Beach Access,
  Restricted Parking)
  As is the case with all shelling beaches, this one is best at low tide. Parking is by permit only, but it is well worth a bike ride to explore this beach.
Theoretically, you can wade all around Tarpon Bay. Walking around all
the mangroves that jut into the Bay, with clumps of sharp oysters clinging
to their roots, renders suitable footwear imperative (See Chapter 3).

Turner's Beach at Blind Pass (Public Beach Access, No Parking
  Restrictions, Rest Room, See description under Gulf beaches)
  Shellers tend to neglect the Bay side of this area, but off-season shellers
cannot afford to do so. At low tide, you can actually walk to some of the
little islands, where surely you will find the highly-prized King's Crown
buried in the "muck"—frequently near clumps of oysters, since they are
particularly fond of them. Look carefully for the little points, for they may
be all that is visible. We have also found large Horse Conchs and Whelks
while wading in this area during the summer months.

North Captiva

As we indicated earlier, you do not want to risk swimming across Redfish Pass to reach this island! However, a half-day excursion around low tide in a rented boat can be extremely rewarding. A short path leads to the Gulf side, where you can enjoy a picnic lunch, a refreshing swim, and some good shelling. The exposed flats on the Bay side are fine areas to explore for large Whelks, Horse Conchs, and Sunray Venus clams.

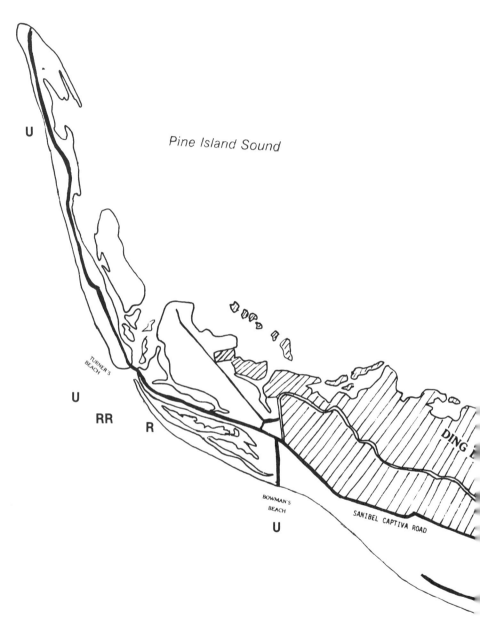

Pine Island Sound

U

U

RR

R

TURNER'S BEACH

BOWMAN'S BEACH

U

SANIBEL CAPTIVA ROAD

DING

U   ... UNRESTRICTED PARKING
R   ... RESTRICTED PARKING
RR... RESTROOM FACILITIES

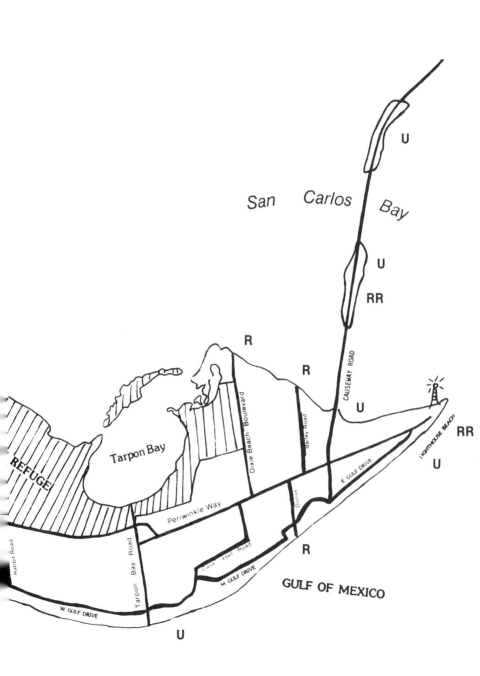

San Carlos Bay

U

U

RR

R

R

Causeway Road

U

REFUGE

Tarpon Bay

Dixie Beach Boulevard

Bailey Road

LIGHTHOUSE BEACH

RR

U

E GULF DRIVE

Periwinkle Way

Dunlix

Rabbit Road

Tarpon Bay Road

Casa Ybel Road

M GULF DRIVE

R

GULF OF MEXICO

W GULF DRIVE

U

CHAPTER 3

EQUIPMENT AND ATTIRE

The Compleat Sheller

For some people, an overriding passion for equipment often exceeds their interest in the activity for which it is intended. There are, of course, some articles of equipment that are highly recommended for shelling.

1. **Hat** Some sort of head covering is essential, especially during the summer months, if you plan to spend any amount of time exposed to the lethal rays of the sun. After all, you do not want to remember this vacation as the time when you collapsed on Captiva.

2. **Sunscreen** A sunscreen (as opposed to tanning lotions and oils) is also highly recommended. You will still get a tan; you just won't burn as well.

3. **Footwear** Unless your feet are remarkably well calloused from years of karate, you will want to protect them from sharp bits of shells. Also, if you are wading, there may be various creatures you would rather not meet in bare feet!

    Some people like the net-type footwear with rubber soles. The sand filters out quite nicely from these inexpensive beach shoes. However, such footwear is not at all good on the Bay side; whatever is not laced on to your feet will slip off in the mud and ooze. Old sneakers are generally the most satisfactory footwear.

4. **Container** You will definitely need something in which to carry your shells. Paper bags are no good at all, for wet shells break right through them. Plastic bags are fine, and so are plastic buckets. You can also cut off (diagonally) the top part of any gallon plastic container that has a handle. Some people like net bags, although these will begin to smell after a while and need to be washed out periodically. A number of shellers favor a kind of apron that has countless pockets. Having both arms free for shelling is a distinct advantage; having the apron smell is not an advantage.

5. **Digging Implements** If you want to dig on an exposed sand bar, or wherever you think the receding tide may have left buried treasure, you do need some sort of tool. A local hardware store will have various metal implements with claws at one end. The long ones require little bending; the short ones involve more exercise. A sturdy serving spoon can be useful — so can an ice cream scoop or a garden trowel. Necessity is the mother of invention, and the imagination of devoted shellers knows no limits!

6. **Light**	If a low tide is at the crack of dawn, or after sunset, you will need a light. Some lanterns cast a powerful beam, as do larger flashlights. Bear in mind the fact that you need a light not only to find shells, but also to avoid breaking an ankle in some pothole left by young sand castle architects!
7. **Winter Weather**	Yes, alas, we do have a winter in Florida. If it's bitter cold in Ohio, the chances are good that it will not be 80° on Sanibel. Early-morning shellers will want to be bundled up when they hit the beaches. A windbreaker (over a warm sweater) is both light and practical. Many shellers wear rubber boots over warm socks. Bare feet, or feet clad only in old sneakers or "net" shoes, soon become numb in the water.
8. **Summer Weather**	During the summer and early fall, there is often very little breeze. Early in the morning, at sunset, and on humid days the "No-See-Ums" are out in force — and with a vengeance. Their incessant biting drives shellers off the beach very quickly. You will want to be armed with a bug spray. Actually, we have found baby oil to be the most effective defense. The No-See-Ums land on your oily arms and legs — and promptly drown. You may come off the beach looking like a walking bug cemetery, but at least you will not be covered with bites.
	One visitor referred to these minute insects as "piranhas with wings" — a very apt description! However, it may be consoling to know that No-See-Ums do have some redeeming social value: they prey on mosquitoes.

THE SANIBEL STOOP AND THE SANIBEL SHUFFLE
(See poem on back cover)

The "Sanibel Stoop" refers to the exceedingly poor posture of those who may spend too much time bending over for shells. It is normally not a permanent condition, but it can be extremely painful. We know of one man who just couldn't straighten up. A local chiropractor made a house call to the beach in this emergency. For those who have bad backs, or wish to avoid getting one, bending over from the waist is not recommended. Genuflect gracefully instead.

The "Sanibel Shuffle," on the other hand, is something that you will definitely want to acquire when wading in our waters — especially in warm weather. Stingrays (see Chapter 8) are very partial to the shallow waters on both sides of the Islands. They will come right up to the edge of the water. or they will lie hidden in mud and sand. They are ugly creatures of such a nondescript color that it is difficult to see one until it actually moves.

Everyone says that stingrays fear you more than you fear them. We have stepped on so many of these "fearful" creatures, and felt so many of them wiggle in the sand under our feet, that we tend to be skeptical about their temerity. In any event, shuffle along when you wade, being certain to let stingrays know that you are there. If, by some great misfortune, the barb of a stingray's tail becomes lodged in your foot, you should seek medical attention immediately.

CHAPTER 4

UNIVALVES

The Vigorous Vacuum Cleaner

Many collectors are especially partial to univalves. Generally spiral in shape, these shells are often extremely colorful and artfully decorated. So far as bivalves are concerned, the snails that inhabit univalve shells are deadly indeed. They are generally voracious, aggressive carnivores that prey on bivalves — and other univalves as well. Since marine snails are so partial to clams, one has to wonder about the origin of the expression, "happy as a clam."

ATLANTIC AUGER (1-1½ ")

Augers are slender, spike-like shells with many whorls. You can easily find them on our Gulf beaches at any time of the year. Their shape and their abundance make them ideal for shell craft.

Augers are carnivorous sand dwellers that, presumably, feed on marine worms. They resemble Cones in that they have a harpoon-like tooth which injects venom into their prey. Of course, Augers also have enemies; starfish like to "swallow" them.

Our Atlantic Auger is pale gray with bands of purplish gray and reddish brown. Some specimens are almost white. Most have about 15 whorls, each one of which has 20-25 axial ribs. Fortunately, you will not have to resort to a magnifying glass to count axial ribs. When you find Augers, you will have no problem in identifying them.

WEST INDIAN BUBBLE (½-1")

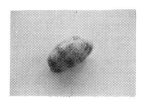

Bubble snails are very common in warm seas. The shells, which look rather rolled up, are usually light and fairly fragile. This carnivorous snail likes to burrow in the sand, where it swallows small mollusks alive. The victim is then thoroughly crushed by means of limy plates in the snail's gizzard.

You can always find an empty Bubble shell along the edge of Sanibel's Gulf beaches. The smooth, rather shiny shell is usually reddish brown or grayish brown. The aperture is extremely long, and rounded at both ends. Bubbles are used very effectively in shell craft. We know one woman who makes entire bouquets of pussy willows by attaching these shells to long strands of wire.

BUTTON SHELL (¼ - ½ ″)

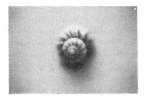

More formally referred to as an Atlantic Modulus, our common little Button shell belongs to a family whose members resemble miniature Top shells. You can always find an unoccupied Florida Button on our Gulf beaches.

This knobby little shell has 3 or 4 whorls and a very low spire. The sculpture of radial ridges, and thick vertical ribs on the upper half of the shell, is extremely well defined. The basic color is creamy white, spotted with brown. Many specimens found on the beach have been bleached white.

CANTHARUS SHELLS

Small Cantharus snails are actually members of the great Whelk family. They are generally not very prepossessing in appearance, and some specimens are considered real pests to commercial oyster beds. You can easily find both specimens listed below throughout the year on our Gulf beaches, at low tide.

False Drill (1 ″)

This shell has 6 whorls and about 8 very distinct vertical ribs on the main body whorl. While the color of this specimen is rather variable, it is commonly a grayish white with brown spots.

Tinted Cantharus (½ - 1 ¼ ″)

This small, rather nondescript shell is extremely common on our Gulf beaches. We often see them in shallow pools of water left by a receding tide. The color of this shell varies somewhat, but it is frequently reddish brown, mottled with white. The rather sturdy shell has 5 or 6 whorls, and vertical ridges are crossed by numerous spiral rings.

CERITHS

Ceriths belong to a very large family of snails called Horn Shells. These tiny snails have many whorls on their spiral-shaped shells. They prefer shallow water, where they feed on detritus. They, in turn, serve as food for sandpipers.

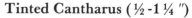

Florida Cerith (1 - 1 ½ ″)

Like the Atlantic Auger, whose shape it somewhat resembles, the Florida Cerith is always in evidence at the edge of the water on our Gulf beaches. This brownish, spiral-shaped shell is spotted with tiny white dots. It has about 10 whorls, with beaded spiral cords between them.

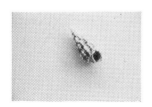

Fly-Specked Cerith (1 ″)

This shell has 8 or 9 axial ribs with little beads on them. There are also several thin, spiral threads with little brown speckles — hence the name, ''Fly-Specked.'' The basic off-white color of the shell is rather obscured by all the brown dots.

Ivory Cerith (1 ″)

The Ivory Ceriths, or Ivory Horn Shells, that we have found on Sanibel's Gulf beaches are little more than half an inch long. The creamy white, spiral-shaped shell has splashes of brown. There are 6 or 7 rounded whorls, each with 4-6 rows of tiny raised beads.

CONES

There are some 5,000 species of cone-shaped snails, the vast majority of which live in the warm waters of the Pacific and Indian Oceans. Collectors are always eager to find cones, for they are extremely colorful. In fact, some of the most valuable shells in the world are cones.

You are most likely to find two kinds of cones on Sanibel, and both are lovely additions to any collection. Like other cones, our Alphabet and Florida Cones possess a characteristic that is highly unusual among mollusks: a harpoon-like device whose venom numbs both prey and enemies. Once the "harpoon" has been used, another replaces it.

We have never heard of a sheller's being harpooned by a cone on our Islands. Should such a thing occur, however, the venom of these cones is not fatal. In any event, handle live specimens with care!

Alphabet Cone (1 - 3″)

This is one of our most beautiful shells, and collectors are very happy to return with a fine specimen. You are most likely to find an Alphabet Cone on a Gulf beach in high season, or after a good storm. Those that you find washed up on the beach are probably not live shells.

Some call this shell a Chinese Alphabet Cone because of the regular rows of brown or orange characters that go around the smooth white shell. The color of a live Alphabet Cone tends to be much darker, and such specimens should be handled gingerly. So far as the animal is concerned, you are just another predator.

Florida Cone (1 - 2″)

A smaller relative of the Alphabet Cone, the Florida Cone is still a very colorful shell. The snail's poisonous eating habits are similar to those of the Alphabet Cone, and it, too, is most often found on the Gulf side in high season or after a fine storm. The shell's basic cream color is decorated with blotches or bands of yellow or orange. As with the Alphabet Cone, darker color indicates that you may have a live specimen in your hand.

Jasper Cone (½ - 1″)

This sturdy little cone has quite a prominent spire. The body of the shell has many very distinct and evenly spaced spiral lines. The color can be quite variable. A rather creamy color with brownish blotches and spots is fairly common.

Stearns' Cone (¼ - ½″)

It is very easy to confuse this cone with the Jasper Cone. In fact, some authorities feel that it is a subspecies of the Jasper Cone. However, there are some small differences.

The spire of Stearns' Cone is far less pronounced. Also, the spiral lines at the base of the shell are much more defined than those further up. The brownish color of the shell is decorated with white spots.

DOVE SHELLS

There are some 400 kinds of Dove shells throughout the world. All are small, and many are true miniatures. They range in size from one tenth of an inch to one inch. Dove shells prefer shallow water, where they feed peacefully on algae. These shells are frequently used in making shell jewelry.

Common Dove Shell
(about 0.3″)

The body whorl of this tiny, but heavy, shell has some 12 spiral ridges. The outer lip is thick towards the middle, a common characteristic of Dove shells, and has about a dozen minute teeth. The color varies quite a bit. Most specimens are white with splashes of brown, while other samples may appear rather mottled with yellow or orange.

Rusty Dove Shell
(about 0.3″)

This specimen is more difficult to find than the Common Dove Shell. It is about the same size, but thinner and less squat. Also, the body whorl is smooth, and often polished. The basic yellow or white color is quite spotted with brown.

FIGHTING CONCH (2 - 4″)

The Fighting Conch (pronounced "konk") belongs to an interesting family of highly aggressive snails. Like so many of our shells, this specimen is more prevalent during the high season, or after a storm. However, you can still find good Fighting Conchs in "muck" and mud on the Bay side of the Islands during the summer.

The carnivorous Fighting Conch snail is rather imaginative when it comes to food. He can enjoy a royal feast at the expense of a much larger animal by wedging himself right into the opening of his prey. Unable to close his protective door, the victim is utterly vulnerable.

The exterior of the Fighting Conch is brown, while the color of the interior lip is orange-brown or red-brown. As is the case with all shells, the color is more vivid if the shell is live.

Since young (Immature) Fighting Conchs do not bear that close a resemblance to mature specimens, we have included a picture — lest you think you have discovered a new species. Should you find an albino, by all means call the local newspapers!

HORSE CONCH
The carnivorous Horse Conch is our State Shell, and also the largest shell you can find in Florida. Exposed sand bars and mud flats are good places to look for a very large, aggressive snail that loves to eat other snails and bivalves by sucking them out of their shells. The Horse Conch snail is edible, but most Americans do not care for its peppery flavor.

Horse Conch (up to 24″)
You will generally find very young Horse Conchs at the water's edge on any Gulf beach. At half an inch, they are orange or yellow. Large, mature Horse Conchs are covered with brownish material, which may be cleaned off to reveal a much lighter shade. Once again, high season, or after a storm, is the best time to find this shell.

Friends of ours always seem to find large Horse Conchs off Captiva Island, around the flats. We found a 14″ specimen on the Bay side of North Captiva in the middle of the summer.

Knobless Wonder (See Chapter 7)

JUNONIA (See Chapter 7)

Cayenne Keyhole Limpet
(½ - 1″)

There are over 500 species of limpets in the world. Sanibel's common Cayenne Keyhole Limpet, also called a "Chinese Hat," belongs to one major group of these vegetarian snails.

In some parts of the world, larger varieties of limpets are eaten raw, or with a sauce, or perhaps cooked in a soup. Apparently, one should not eat too many limpets at one sitting, for the snails have some very hard teeth in their dental apparatus. Since these teeth are not digestible, a quantity of them may form a hard ball and cause considerable intestinal distress. This is not at all hard to believe when one realizes that these vegetarian snails feed on algae-covered rocks. The constant rasping of the teeth of generations of Keyhole Limpets is definitely a factor in the erosion of shoreline rocks.

The hole near the apex of the shell is what distinguishes Keyhole Limpets from "true" limpets. However, this keyhole performs a very useful function. Keyhole Limpets draw in water underneath the shell. The water passes over the gills, and waste matter is expelled through the keyhole.

"Chinese Hat" is a very appropriate name for the Cayenne Keyhole Limpet that you can easily find on Sanibel's Gulf beaches throughout the year. The shell has numerous radial ribs, every third or fourth rib being larger than those in between. The interior of the shell is white, but the white exterior is decorated with broad, blackish radial stripes. These dark stripes are, of course, less evident in specimens that have been exposed to the sun for very long.

King's Crown (1 - 4")

This highly-prized shell is also called a Florida Crown Conch. Unfortunately, the King's Crown is in great demand by collectors, shell crafters, even jewelry makers. This demand is due to the fact that the King's Crown displays great variation in form and color (basically white with brown bands of various hues).

Some specimens have no spines at all, while others may have one, two, even three rows of spines. Experts say that these variations are caused by both heredity and environment.

We have had no luck at all in finding good specimens on Gulf beaches. However, we have always discovered colonies on the Bay side of the Islands at any time of the year, during a low tide.

If you want to find a good King's Crown, go where the "muck" is; they seem to thrive in it. Since these snails love oysters, look for those telltale spines wherever you see clumps of oysters. All the little mangrove islands on the Bay side are also good sites, for oysters like to cling to mangrove roots. Since Kings' Crowns are all covered with very dark muck in such areas, it is very easy to walk right by one if you are not looking for the little spines.

MARGINELLAS

Most Marginellas (margin shells) are extremely small, and those that you find on our Islands throughout the year are likely to be miniatures — shells no larger than half an inch at maturity. The beauty of these very glossy little shells has made them extremely popular with collectors and shell crafters.

When univalves are very glossy in their natural state, this usually indicates that the mantle of the living snail covered most of the outer shell while the animal was crawling along. This is true of Moon Snails and Olives, for example. Actually, Marginella snails do far more than crawl along the bottom; they seem to glide over it at a remarkable pace for such a tiny animal.

Common Atlantic Marginella (¼ - ½ ″)

This glossy little shell is the most common Marginella, and therefore the one you are most likely to find - and be able to see with the naked eye. The spire is very low, and the aperture is very narrow. The inner lip has 4 tiny folds. The basic color of this shell is a very light, golden yellow.

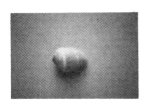

Orange Marginella (½ - ¾ ″)

This specimen is supposed to be uncommon. However, since we found two in one day, shellers may have good luck on Sanibel. The glossy shell is bright orange, with 2 thin white bands going around the middle.

Teardrop Marginella (0.1″)

Many shellers confuse this miniature specimen with the Common Atlantic Marginella. Since the Teardrop Marginella is frequently no more than one tenth of an inch, its size (or lack of it) should aid in identification. Moreover, the glossy shell is white. You may need a magnifying glass to see 3 little folds on the inner lip.

MOON SNAILS

Moon Snails love to burrow in the sand, probably because they also love to feast on several clams a day. The little round holes that you often see in various bivalve shells may well have been made by a greedy Moon Snail. (On the other hand, you may see a little round hole in a Moon Snail, indicating that some sea creature did unto him as he did unto others!)

At low tide, these snails leave a nice, meandering trail on sand bars. You may also see a little "collar" of sand all stuck together. Moon Snails leave their eggs in these sand collars. Should you find one, you may also find a good specimen in the vicinity.

Baby's Ear (See Chapter 7)

Cat's Eye (½ - 3½")

One annoying thing about the Cat's Eye is that many shellers also call it a Shark's Eye. Frankly, we think that this shell resembles the eye of a shark far more than it does the eye of a cat. But then, how would one list another Moon Snail, called a Shark's Eye?

In any event, a Cat's Eye is generally gray in color, although you may also find some tan ones. We have had good luck in finding very large Cats' Eyes at the outer edge of exposed sand bars at any time of the year. Often, they are just washed up on the beach, and still retain a high gloss if they have not been there too long.

Shark's Eye (1½ -2") (Atlantic Natica)

This beautiful shell is harder to find than the Cat's Eye, although its feeding habits are quite similar. We have generally found Sharks' Eyes washed up on Gulf beaches during the winter months. The cream or light tan background is very artistically decorated with a wide beige band, and either zigzag or wavy brown lines. The lovely Shark's Eye is a most welcome addition to any collection.

MUREX

Members of the Murex family are characterized by very strong, rather spiny shells. Once again, a carnivorous snail inhabits live specimens and preys on bivalves. The suction of the snail's strong foot, coupled with the prying motion of the outer lip of the shell, forces open clams and oysters for the snail's delectation.

Like Pen shells and scallops, Murex shells have had their moment of historical glory. In ancient times, Mediterranean societies vied for control of the profitable trade in purple dye. A particular gland in most species of Murex snails produces a yellowish fluid, which reportedly smells like rotten cabbage. When exposed to the sun, the fluid turns purple. The Phoenicians gained a monopoly of this product by developing a secret process for removing the fluid from the mollusk. Tyrian purple cloth was so valuable, and in such great demand, that the Phoenicians could command outrageous prices for it. After the Romans had conquered the ancient Mediterranean world, they decreed that only the Roman emperor could wear Tyrian purple robes. (One has to assume that the stench of rotting cabbage did not persist.)

Apple Murex (1½ - 3½")
This rather rough, knobby shell is especially common on our Gulf beaches during the winter months, but you can also find it at other times of the year. The Apple Murex is quite a colorful specimen with a mixture of light orange, yellow, and dark brown markings.

Lace Murex (1 - 3")
The dainty Lace Murex is much more spiny than its colorful relative, an attribute that may atone for its own general lack of color. Most specimens that you find will be white, although some may be a dull brown. The pointed tip is pink.

NASSA MUD SNAILS

The large family of Nassa Mud Snails is widely distributed, but most species prefer warm waters. These tiny snails are extremely active scavengers. They do not actually "smell" decaying fish, crabs, etc.; rather, they "taste" them. The water's delicious flavors of decaying flesh are drawn in through the snail's siphon and passed over its taste organ. Within a few seconds, the snail is on its way to a lovely feast. If the feeding habits of these scavenger snails are somewhat distasteful, one has to remember that their singular appetites help to keep exposed mud flats clean. Clearly the best place to look for these scavengers is on exposed mud flats, in the area around dead fish and crabs.

Common Eastern Nassa (0.5″)

This sturdy little shell has about 5 whorls, and its spire is pointed. There are 12 beaded axial ribs. The color of the shell is usually white and rather mottled with gray and brown. However, the Common Eastern Nassa is so abundant, and it is such a variable specimen, that samples found on different beaches may exhibit different color patterns.

Sharp-Knobbed Nassa (0.5″)

A true miniature shell, the Sharp-Knobbed Nassa is rather shiny, with about 5 whorls and strong vertical ribs crossed by little ridges. The color is generally white, often with brown spots.

NUTMEG (1 - 1½ ″)

It is rather refreshing to find such a lovely shell, inhabited by a snail that may be a vegetarian! The Nutmeg derives its name from the fact that its rather rough texture, and to some degree its shape, bear a resemblance to the nutmeg seed. Some authorities claim that the living snail is carnivorous, while others assert that it is a vegetarian. Perhaps the eating habits depend upon the particular species — or the mood of the snail.

This very sturdy shell is especially visible on our Gulf beaches during the winter months. Various shades of brown are attractively arranged in spiral bands and lengthwise stripes. The Nutmegs that you will find are generally intact, thanks to the toughness of the shell.

OLIVES

Collectors favor olives, for the shell is usually quite glossy. The reason for such a high gloss is the fact that the carnivorous snail's body covers most of the shell while it moves along. Many specimens that you find washed up on the beach still retain this porcelain-like finish.

Dwarf Olive (about 0.2″)
You may need a magnifying glass both to find this miniature and to enjoy its glossy beauty. Many of the specimens washed ashore are light brown in color.

Lettered Olive (1 - 3″)
This shell derives its name from the pattern of dark markings. The Indians used to make necklaces out of these olives. The Lettered Olive is one of our most attractive shells, and you can find one at any time of the year — especially on Gulf beaches. Olives are usually a glossy beige to brown color with zigzag markings going around the shell. A live olive has an especially high gloss, but there really is no need to take a live one when so many other fine specimens are available. Some olives are gray, and seem less attractive. A golden olive is a rare find for the collector!

You will often find "headless" olives. If they are good specimens in other respects, they may well come in handy for shell craft.

Rice Olive (about 0.3″)

The living snail in this miniature shell is carnivorous, and likes to burrow in the sand. The glossy shell, which somewhat resembles a grain of rice, is white.

OYSTER DRILLS

Oyster drills all belong to the Murex family of very active, carnivorous snails. Their small shells are generally sturdy, and often quite spiny. Unlike starfish, these voracious snails do not have the patience to pry open the valves of an oyster. They simply drill a hole right through the shell. Thoughts of oyster drills must give oystermen horrible nightmares, for these snails wreak havoc in oyster beds and are responsible for millions of dollars worth of damage every year.

Several kinds of oyster drills are very common in the shallow waters around our Islands. However, it is extremely difficult for amateur shellers to tell one from another or, for that matter, to differentiate between any one of them and a baby Murex. Therefore, we have included no photographs of the first three drills listed below. The following is a brief description of these particular drills, accompanied by sketches.

Atlantic Oyster Drill (about 0.7″)

Perhaps the most destructive of the drills, this snail ranges from Nova Scotia to Florida, and has been introduced elsewhere as well. It is rather dirty gray in color.

Gulf Oyster Drill (about 0.7″)

The sturdy, yellowish-gray shell of this snail is very similar to that of the Atlantic Oyster Drill. However, its outer lip is thicker, and its opening is smaller.

Tampa Oyster Drill (about 1″)

What differentiates this shell from those of the two preceding drills is the crisscross pattern of sharp axial ribs and sturdy spiral threads.

Sharp-Ribbed Drill (about 0.5″)

This drill is very common in the shallow waters of western Florida. Fortunately, it is not at all hard to identify. The pinkish-gray shell does indeed appear to be very "Sharp-Ribbed."

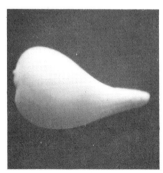

Paper Fig (2 - 4″)

The snail in the pear-shaped Paper Fig likes the sand. As it crawls along under the water, the fleshy part of the snail nearly covers the shell, thus protecting its rather fragile home.

The Paper Fig is such a thin shell that its arrival, intact, on Gulf beaches during the winter months seems miraculous. Since this snail is extremely partial to Sea Urchins, it is not uncommon to find both predator and prey washed up at the same time.

Nearly all the Paper Figs that we have found are off-white in color. The larger specimens frequently have light brown areas, especially on the glossy interior. Viewed from the exterior, these areas look almost purple. You may find specimens in which you can barely make out many light brown spots. Do not confuse the Paper Fig with the Pear Whelk.

Angulate Periwinkle (½ - 1½")

This specimen, which you can easily find on our Islands throughout the year, is a "true" Periwinkle. That is, the snail's habitat is always around the shore. The best place to look for an Angulate Periwinkle (also known as a Southern Periwinkle) is on the Bay side, attached to mangrove roots and wharf pilings.

True Periwinkles feed on microscopic algae. The fact that a number of species are able to live out of the water for extended periods of time has caused some experts to believe that many of today's land snails evolved from ancient members of this family.

While a number of Sanibel's streets are named after shells — especially those on the eastern end of the Island — Periwinkle Way is, apparently, not one of them. A long-time resident assured us that Sanibel's main thoroughfare was named after the charming little flower that once grew in profusion along the sides of this road.

The color of this smooth, thin, yet strong shell varies from brownish purple to gray — with very dark, oblique markings. The shell has 6 or 7 whorls with a sharp point, and is marked by numerous minute spiral lines.

SCOTCH BONNET
(See Chapter 7)

Simnia (about ¾ ")

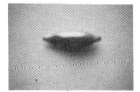

Simnia snails live in warm waters on Sea Whips and Sea Fans. It is believed that these yellow or purplish mollusks may possess the remarkable ability to match their color to their environment. For example, those that you find on wine-colored Sea Whips will be the same color, while those that you see on yellow Sea Whips will be yellow.

If you would like to find some of these brightly colored, glossy little shells, look carefully among the branches of Sea Whips that have recently been washed ashore on our Gulf beaches. In addition to Ponderous Arks and other shells, you should also be able to find Simnia shells.

SLIPPER SHELLS

There are many kinds of Slipper shells on our Gulf beaches throughout the year. Children delight in discovering these little "Indian Boats," or "Canoes," names derived from the little seat on the inside. This same seat causes some to refer to these shells as "Quarterdecks." As Quarterdecks, the shells actually have a certain commercial value. Every year, tons of empty shells are scattered on the ocean floor so that embryo oysters can settle on them.

Adult Slipper shells do not move about very much. In fact, they tend to remain in one spot until they die. Some species merely sit on the shells of others and form chains. Others, like the Flat and Convex Slipper, like to attach themselves to the interiors of dead shells. You might even find dozens of them on the shell of a horseshoe crab.

Common Atlantic Slipper Shell (1½″)

This shell often has brown streaks on a white background. However, there really is a very wide range of color in all Slipper shells. Some, for example, may be entirely brown, or almost orange.

Convex Slipper Shell (½″)

The smallest member of the family, the Convex Slipper Shell is very strongly arched, and the brown apex reminds one of a hook. The basic color is reddish brown. You will often find this specimen attached to other shells. Turn over a horseshoe crab that has washed onto the beach; you can often find dozens of these little shells attached on the inside.

Flat Slipper Shell (1″)

The main difference between this specimen and other members of the family is that it is relatively flat, as opposed to being arched.

Spotted Slipper Shell (1″)

The exterior of this shell is generally marked with brown, or chocolate-chip spots.

Thorny Slipper Shell (1″)

The specimens that we have found tend to be brown. However, as with all Slipper shells, there is considerable variation in color. The exterior of this shell has irregular ridges, spiny or thorny.

COMMON SUNDIAL
(See Chapter 7)

Sculptured Top Shell (½ - 1″)

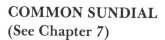

This lovely little shell really does resemble a toy top. Flat on the bottom, it has 5 or 6 whorls and is artfully decorated with revolving rows of minute beads. The basic off-white color is heavily mottled with reddish brown. Unlike so many snails, this one is a vegetarian.

TULIPS

Tulips belong to the same family as Horse Conchs and, a bit more technically, are called Tulip Conchs. Like Horse Conchs, Tulip snails are highly aggressive carnivores, enjoying both bivalves and other snails. Both kinds of Tulips are common during the winter months, and we have also found some good specimens on the Bay side in the summer.

Banded Tulip (1 - 4″)

The Banded Tulip derives its name from the very thin, dark spiral lines that form bands around the shell. The shells are often a pearly gray, although you can find specimens with splashes of tan, green, or orange. A predominantly yellow Banded Tulip is a very good find!

44

True Tulip (3 - 8″)

The True Tulip is less common than its banded relative, and thus more rewarding to find. During the high season, it is not uncommon to find small (2-4″) True Tulips washed up on our Gulf beaches or nestled in the sand at low tide. The True Tulip is always a colorful addition to your collection.

The color of these extremely handsome shells is quite variable. Specimens found on the Bay side tend to be dark brown or dark green, with generous splashes of dark brown. Shells that are primarily red or orange are somewhat less common. However, they do appear on the Gulf side during the winter months. As with the Banded Tulip, a yellow specimen would be an extraordinarily good find.

Chestnut Turban (1 - 1½″)

Turbans are generally rather sturdy, top-shaped shells that bear a strong resemblance to the turbans worn in some societies. Varieties of Turban shells are found in tropical waters throughout the world, and many have been used for decorative purposes. The colorful operculum of one species, for example, is used in south Pacific island jewelry.

We have had good luck in finding Chestnut Turbans on Sanibel's Gulf beaches. As is the case with so many shells, Turbans are more plentiful during the winter months. The snail that once inhabited this shell was herbivorous — quite unlike most of its highly aggressive fellow snails.

The top-shaped Chestnut Turban has 5 or 6 whorls, decorated with beads. The color is light brown, generously blotched with darker brown.

TURRIDS

Some texts refer to this large family of "Turridae" snails as Turrets. In any event, Turrids have been around for millions of years and include hundreds of living and fossil forms. Even experts find it difficult to identify various species of these spindle-shaped gastropods. We have included two fairly common specimens found on our beaches — and pray that their identification is accurate! Incidentally, to make matters even more confusing, both are called "Drillia."

Oyster Turrid (0.3″)

Also called an Oyster Drillia, this strong, spindle-shaped shell has 7 or 8 whorls and some 20 axial ribs that are faintly beaded and crossed by spiral threads. The color of this shell is usually reddish brown.

Sanibel Turrid (0.8″)

Also known as the Sanibel Drillia, this specimen is not common at all and appears to be limited to the west coast of Florida. While the shell resembles the Oyster Turrid, it is generally larger. Moreover, it has about 8 whorls and only 9 axial ribs. The color is reddish brown.

Ivory Tusk (1 - 1½″)

The only shell in this chapter that is not a gastropod (snail), the Ivory Tusk is in a class by itself. It is a primitive mollusk and has no head, eyes, hearts, or gills. Scaphopods include nearly 1,000 species of living Tusk shells throughout the world.

Somewhat curved and open at both ends, Tusk or "Tooth" shells live in the sand, often at greath depths, with their smaller end uppermost. The foot, which is extremely well suited for burrowing, protrudes from the larger end. Tiny one-celled animals are the main staple for Tusk shells. Once drawn into the shell, along with water, these minute organisms are crushed by the animal's dental apparatus. Many species of fish find Tusk shells quite delectable, and the ubiquitous Hermit Crab often makes his home inside an empty specimen.

The best way to find an Ivory Tusk is to scratch around piles of shell scrap on a Gulf beach. The tapering, cylindrical shell is slightly curved. Usually, it is pure white in color, and the surface is smooth. Some specimens may be quite glossy, while others may be rather dull and chalky.

Angulate Wentletrap (½ - 1″)

Wentletraps, or "Staircase Shells," are favorites among collectors, for they are particularly graceful specimens endowed with magnificent sculpture. There are over 200 living species in all seas (around 11 on Sanibel), and perhaps as many fossil species as well.

Identifying various specimens requires considerable expertise, and involves such tasks as counting the number and shape of axial ribs, noting the angle of the spire, and being well versed in all the arcana of Wentletraps.

Wentletraps are carnivorous snails. Some species feed voraciously on Sea Anemones. If Sea Anemones are not available, Wentletraps will attack just about anything else, including much larger snails.

The lovely Angulate Wentletrap is a specimen that amateur shellers are most likely to find on our Gulf beaches throughout the year. Piles of shell scrap are good hunting grounds for such small shells. The rather glossy, white shell has about 6 whorls, each with some 10 blade-like ribs.

47

WHELKS

Whelks (pronounced "Welks") are probably the largest (over 2,000 species) family of marine snails in the world, ranging from polar regions to tropical climes. These large snails are extremely partial to hard-shelled clams. They kill their victims by enveloping them in a deadly embrace, and then tearing them apart. One can almost always find a Whelk, for he is a survivor 'par excellence.'

Scientists say that Whelks have been around for some 60 million years. They were a major staple for Florida's Indians, and you can still find large old shells in Indian burial mounds on Sanibel. Whelk shells were also used for everything from soup ladles to deadly weapons.

The Whelk's natural defense against extinction is a remarkable ability to reproduce. You will often find their egg casings washed up on the beach. These resemble a long, coiled snake whose mother inadvertently mated with an accordian.

Lightning Whelk (2 - 14″)

You can easily find a good Lightning Whelk on our Gulf beaches during the winter, or after a storm. During the off-season, however, we have had very good luck in finding both kinds of Whelks on the Bay side of the Islands.

The Lightning Whelk is rather perverse. Unlike most univalves, it whorls to the left rather than to the right. A very rare find indeed is an even more perverse Whelk that whorls to the right! Lightning Whelks are generally beige to yellow on the outside with brown, vertical stripes that remind one of streaks of lightning. Inside, the shell may be a yellowish brown, pink or even purple. Very large older specimens tend to lose their color entirely and become creamy white.

Pear Whelk (2 ½ - 4″)

The Pear Whelk is somewhat less common than the Lightning Whelk, and never attains great size. Moreover, the Pear Whelk is not perverse; it follows the crowd and whorls to the right. This shell has smooth shoulders, with no little points on top. On the surface, it really has little in common with the Lightning Whelk, other than its passion for clams.

The rather pear-shaped shell is generally creamy white with splashes of tan or yellow. Do not confuse this specimen with the less-colorful Paper Fig, which is also pear shaped.

Worm Shell (3 - 8″)

Our discussion of many noble, colorful univalves ends with the lowly Worm Shell. (In subsequent editions, we may list it under the more charitable name, "Old Maid's Curl"). Few sources have much to say about the Worm Shell. It is almost always on the beach, or in Bay-side mud flats. You may even find several of them together in shallow water, all tangled up.

This strange creature really does resemble a worm rather than a mollusk. However, the animal is thoroughly snail-like with tentacles and eyes on its head and a toothed tongue. Live specimens often lead a very comfortable life inside a sponge.

A sturdy shell, the early whorls of the Worm Shell are tightly coiled, forming the head. As the shell grows, subsequent whorls are very loosely coiled. The Worm Shell is generally a creamy beige-brown color. If you display your shells in a printer's tray, this specimen looks just fine dangling out of one of the spaces.

CHAPTER 5

BIVALVES

Carol Cleavage collects cockles.

A French lady once remarked that there are two kinds of people in the world: those who eat, and those who are eaten. It occurred to us that one could apply her perceptive wisdom to the world of univalves and bivalves. We have described the aggressive, imaginative eating habits of many univalve snails that bore holes, pry open, smother in a deadly embrace, or harpoon and inject with venom. Bivalves, which are generally clams, oysters, mussels, and scallops, seem to exist in order to feed univalves, other sea creatures, and voracious mankind in general.

ANGEL WING (See Chapter 7)

ARKS

Experts note that Arks are a very ancient family of clams that go back to the Jurassic period. While these clams are edible, Americans do not usually care for their bitter taste.

Arks tend to have rather strong, boxy, heavy shells that are not especially colorful. Few shellers bother to display many in their collections. Much to their credit, however, Arks are extremely reliable. You can always find them on our Gulf beaches, and they are often used in shell craft.

Cut-Ribbed Ark (3 - 5″)

This shell resembles a Ponderous Ark that was stretched in a tug of war. Those that you find washed up on our Gulf beaches are usually white, having lost any dark outer coating (periostracum) they may once have had.

The sturdy Cut-Ribbed Ark has around 35 radial ribs. You can generally detect at least two fine concentric lines cutting across both the ribs and the grooves. Presumably, this particular feature accounts for the name of this specimen.

Mossy Ark (1 ½ - 2 ½ ″)

Somewhat less common than the Turkey Wing, the Mossy Ark is shaped very much like its more colorful, zebra-striped relative. The outer shell is basically dark brown.

51

Ponderous Ark (1 - 3")

Especially common on Sanibel throughout the year, this bivalve is well named: it is rather heavy, both in appearance and in weight. Some specimens are completely white, but many still retain the black outer covering on all but the beak. It is very common to find both shells intact, in which case you have a good start on making a shell-craft bird.

Transverse Ark (1 - 1½")

The smallest member of the family, the Transverse Ark is just as prevalent as its relatives on our Gulf beaches. It may have only a dozen ribs, and it is generally white. However, live Arks, or those that have not been exposed to the elements for very long, tend to have quite a bit of dark brown or black exterior coating.

Turkey Wing (2 - 3½")

The Turkey Wing really does resemble the wing of a turkey. This bivalve clam is also called a Zebra Ark, for its strong shell is covered with brown, zebra-like stripes. The shell has a perfectly straight hinge line with some 50 small teeth. There are numerous rounded ribs of irregular size.

Broad-Ribbed Cardita (1 - 1½")

Clams of the Cardita family have rather thick shells with very strong, radiating ribs. You can find a Broad-Ribbed Cardita on our Gulf beaches at any time of the year.

Most specimens have about 20 sturdy ribs. The exterior of the shell often exhibits more variety of color than many texts indicate. While sun-bleached specimens may be entirely white, most will be covered with brown or orange spots. A number of these shells appear to be totally orange-brown. Thousands of Broad-Ribbed Carditas are gathered up each year for use in shell craft.

COCKLES

You can find cockles throughout the year on our beaches. Actually, there are over 200 species in seas throughout the world. These edible clams are commonly displayed in European markets.

Cockles are easy to identify, for all are heart-shaped when viewed from either side. This is why many people call them "Heart Clams."

Live cockles are extremely active; they love to leap and squirt. Thanks to a very strong foot, shaped like a sickle, cockles can leap several inches off the bottom. Many shellers have been quite startled by this acrobatic feat. The squirting usually occurs when you pick up a live specimen and the animal quickly withdraws and closes his valves.

Unfortunately, cockles are used so extensively in shell craft that thousands are picked up on Sanibel each year. There really is no need to pick up a live specimen, for the shells, minus the clam, are always colorful and plentiful.

Common Egg Cockle (1 - 2″)

Unlike the other cockles found on Sanibel, the shell of this clam is quite thin and smooth. Moreover, the color is basically white, often with tints of brown or orange. One can imagine that a very small egg might fit nicely into both valves of this cockle.

Giant Atlantic Cockle (1 -5″)

The Vigorous Vacuum Cleaner (chapter 4) loves this particular cockle, the largest found on Sanibel. The strong, rather heavy shell is generally reddish brown, tan, and yellow on the outside with some 32-36 very pronounced radial ribs. The inside color is often a lovely rose.

Prickly Cockle (1 - 2″)

If you feel like counting ribs, this strong shell has 27-31. They are somewhat prickly, as contrasted with those of other cockles. The outside of the shell is generally white, with light pink splashes. The pink color inside the shell is more vivid.

Spiny Paper Cockle (1 - 2″)

At first glance, this small shell bears very little resemblance to other cockles. While it has many radial ribs, they are extremely fine and it would be impossible to count them without the aid of a magnifying glass. Moreover, the shell is thin and not at all sturdy. The shells of other cockles found on Sanibel are invariably quite inflated, whereas that of the Spiny Paper Cockle is quite compressed.

The color of this slightly elongate shell is extremely attractive, both inside and outside. Basically white or pink, it is very heavily mottled with a rosy brown shade.

The thinness of the shell accounts for the word "Paper" in its name. It is more difficult to account for "Spiny." Theoretically, the radial ribs end with very short spines. We have never found one with such spines. However, one always has to bear in mind the fact that shells washed up on the beach and exposed to the elements are bound to suffer from erosion.

Yellow Cockle (1 - 2″)

This very common shell is mostly yellow on the outside, often with pink near the top. The interior is generally white, yellow, or both.

DONAX

Members of this family are sometimes referred to as "wedge clams" because of their shape. Generally small, these brightly colored little clams are always in evidence on our Gulf beaches, where entire colonies wiggle in and out of the sand close to the shore. Some species are used in making soup, but most are not really large enough to be of commerical value. This is just as well, for snails, crabs, and wading birds already take a very heavy toll of these delightful little clams.

Coquina (½ - 1″)

Coquinas inhabit the tide line. Waves toss them up on the wet sand, into which they disappear immediately. They feed rather gently on minute plant and animal matter until a new wave tosses them out again. At low tide, children love to watch these tiny, sturdy clams appear and disappear in the twinkling of an eye.

Coquinas, or "Butterflies," are equipped with an extremely large foot that enables them to perform their disappearing act with remarkable speed.

The wedge-shaped Coquina shells exhibit a veritable rainbow of colors. Some specimens are all white, red, yellow, even purple. Others are decorated with darker rays of color. The variety seems to be infinite.

Giant False Donax (2 -3″)

This specimen is not a member of the Donax family of clams. Since this clam has no relatives on our Islands, we include it here only because of its English name and because, quite frankly, we did not quite know what else to do with it!

The sturdy False Donax, or "False Coquina," is rather triangular in shape. Unlike Coquinas, this clam prefers calm waters near the shore and is not found on the beaches very often. Shellers need not be too disappointed, however, for the Giant False Donax cannot begin to compete with Coquinas in terms of beauty.

The rather large, heavy shell is creamy white on the interior with a purple stain near the beak. The exterior color is somewhat similar, although the shell may be quite covered with a brownish coating (periostracum).

JEWEL BOXES

Young Jewel Boxes attach themselves to rocks, coral, and other shells. While mature specimens swim freely, you can always detect the small scar marking the spot where the shell was once attached.

Little Corrugated Jewel Box (½ - 1")

Good specimens of this small shell appear to be slightly thorny. The exterior color is reddish brown or orange, while the white interior of the upper valve generally has a purple border.

Spiny Jewel Box (1 - 1½")

You can easily find a Spiny Jewel Box washed up on our Gulf beaches at any time of the year. The valves of this thick, white shell are equally plump, and both have 7-9 rows of radial spines. However, the spines of most beach specimens will normally be considerably reduced. The interior of the shell often has blotches of red or purple.

Atlantic Jingle (1 - 2")

Jingles are very thin, colorful, translucent clam shells. Like Pen shells and mussels, they anchor themselves to a solid object by means of their byssus — a tuft of very fine threads. The flat lower valve of these lovely shells has a hole to accommodate the byssus. The upper valve, which is quite inflated, is washed ashore more frequently than the lower valve.

You can almost always find a good color variety of these fragile shells washed up on our Gulf beaches. Basically circular in shape, the shell undergoes certain distortions depending upon the object to which it was once attached. Most Atlantic Jingles are white, black, orange, or gray.

Children delight in finding these colorful little shells, and many people like to make wind chimes with them.

LUCINES

Lucines are quite easy to recognize because of the long muscle scar inside the shell. The foot of a live Lucine is about six times longer than the shell itself. Periodically, the clam's foot pushes out unwanted debris. Housecleaning should be so easy!

Buttercup Lucine (1 - 2½″)

Circular in shape, this rather thin bivalve can be found at any time of the year. The exterior is white, while the interior is tinged with yellow — hence the name, "Buttercup." While not a very exciting shell, the Buttercup Lucine has the advantage of being both plentiful and uniform in shape — attributes that shell crafters appreciate.

Florida Lucine (½ - 1½″)

The Florida Lucine is a somewhat smaller version of the Buttercup, without the yellow rim on the interior — or, for that matter, any particular color at all.

MUSSELS

Mussels are not normally shells that one is particularly eager to add to a collection. Commonly found on the Bay side of the Islands, these sharp-beaked bivalves are not especially colorful.

Mussels are found in all seas, but tend to prefer cool waters. Most species are somewhat pear-shaped with rather iridescent interiors. While many mussels are edible, Americans tend to prefer oysters and clams. In Europe, however, the mussel is farmed quite extensively. Many restaurants in France offer mussels as an appetizer. They may be stuffed or, more frequently, served in a bowl filled with a thin broth — liberally laced with wine, of course!

Atlantic Ribbed Mussel (2 - 4")

This may not be the only kind of mussel that you will find embedded in our mud flats at low tide, but it is certainly a very common specimen. The animal not only prefers brackish water, but actually thrives in a rather polluted habitat.

The shell is rather thin, and derives its name from the many fine, radial ribs. The exterior color is yellowish brown or bluish green, while the interior is white with bluish hues.

Tulip Mussel (1 - 3")

Since this specimen likes to attach itself to other shells, you are most likely to find it washed ashore after a storm. The Tulip Mussel has no ribs, and the exterior of this thin, smooth shell is yellowish brown. Sometimes the white interior is enlivened by blue, pink, or tan stains.

OYSTERS

Oysters, like mussels, are not generally collected with an eye to displaying their shells. However, gathering certain kinds of oysters for pearls, or for human consumption, is quite a different matter!

There are several families of oysters: tree, pearl, and edible. The pearl oysters are of great economic importance, for several tropical species produce precious pearls. When an oyster is irritated by a grain of sand, for example, layers of nacre (mother-of-pearl) coat around the grain and form a pearl — the only gem made by an animal.

Edible oysters can also produce pearls, but these are inferior and have no commercial value. Even pearls from Florida's Atlantic Pearl Oyster are usually far too small to be of any particular value. Thus, if you are looking for pearls, you may have to go to the southern Caribbean to find larger specimens.

Atlantic Wing Oyster (1 - 3")

This shell is also called a "Winged Pearl Oyster," since it belongs to the pearl oyster group. However, you would have to go to Ceylon or Australia to find valuable pearls from this family of oysters.

One wing, or ear, of the shell's hinge is considerably longer than the other. The exterior color of the rather thin shell is brownish purple, and the radial ribs are quite faint. The interior is iridescent.

Eastern Oyster (2 - 6")

This is the oyster that so many of us enjoy eating raw. Commercially, it is our most important bivalve.

American oystermen tend their oyster farms just as carefully as Europeans watch over their mussel farms. Unfortunately, our Eastern Oyster has many enemies other than humans. While a single oyster lays millions of eggs during each spawning season, only a dozen or so ever reach maturity.

Tiny young oysters swim freely, but they must soon settle upon some hard object and remain permanently attached to it. Should they chance to settle in mud, they die. This explains why oystermen scatter tons of broken shells in the beds every year. (Our Slipper shells are especially popular for this purpose).

If the young oyster escapes an early death in the mud, he must cope with starfish and snails (especially the Oyster Drill) for the rest of his life. The starfish is an exceptionally patient predator (see chapter 8).

The larger valve of this oyster looks rather like a long, knobby foot that could only be comfortable in orthopedic shoes. Basically white in color, it is often streaked with generous splashes of purple, while the interior muscle scar is a deep purple. The other valve of the oyster, much smaller and flatter, is often a dull gray color.

PEN SHELLS

These thin, very brittle, fan-shaped shells are extremely common on our Gulf beaches after any kind of storm or disturbance. Pen shell clams are easily uprooted; they prefer sandy bottoms in shallow waters where they attach themselves to small rocks and pebbles by means of extremely fine threads. It is rumored that large ''scallops'' sold in southern markets may often be chunks cut from the muscles of Pen shells.

The rough, often spiny, exterior of Pen shells attracts specimens that like to cling to something. It is not uncommon to find Pen shells encrusted with barnacles, oysters, Slipper shells, and Tube Worms. Moreover, infant Murex shells, and other immature specimens, often seek refuge inside Pen shells, Another rent-free resident is a particular kind of crab that enjoys protection, while feeding on food particles that pass within its orbit.

Although shells have not caused great empires to rise and fall, some species merit a special footnote in history. A Mediterranean species of the common Pen shell enjoyed its finest hour in ancient times.

While it is hard to be very charitable in describing the rather ugly Pen shell, the mollusk does possess one highly-redeeming feature: its byssus. This is the tuft of extremely fine threads with which the bivalve attaches itself to rocks and pebbles. Once dried out and well cleaned, these threads are gold in color and rival the most exquisite spun silk. In ancient times, Mediterranean kings are said to have worn magnificent robes woven from these golden threads. Moreover, there is some speculation that the mythological Golden Fleece was woven from the fine byssal threads of the lowly Pen shell.

Rigid Pen Shell (4 - 8″)

Both valves of this rather ugly mollusk are often washed up on the Islands' Gulf beaches after any kind of storm. The dark, olive-brown color reminds one of the Army, and the shell's general appearance is scarcely enhanced by the presence of some 15 radial rows of spines.

However, the interior break portion of the shell is often magnificent. It is rather like mother-of-pearl, iridescent with its rainbow of colors. Broken fragments of this pearly portion of the shell are almost always in evidence on our Gulf beaches. It is hard to understand why these lovely fragments are not used more extensively in shell craft.

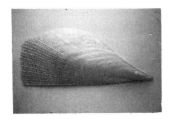

Saw-Toothed Pen Shell   (4 -8″)

Like its spiny relative, the Saw-Toothed Pen Shell would not win any beauty contest. Very similar in both shape and size, this specimen enjoys much more delicate sculpture. Over 30 fine ribs are set close together and adorned with tiny scales. Run a finger over these scales and you will quickly see why this specimen is called "Saw-Toothed." The exterior color of the shell is a light olive brown.

SCALLOPS AND PECTENS

Scallops are probably the most popular bivalves, for they exhibit a remarkably wide variety of color. Collectors enjoy displaying a good color series of each kind of scallop. Lemon-yellow and purple are the rarest colors; orange is also relatively uncommon.

You can always find a good variety of scallops on our Gulf beaches, and it is hard to resist filling your garage with these beautiful shells! The only specimen that you are not likely to find is the highly-prized Lion's Paw (see chapter 7).

There are many kinds of scallop shells, and sometimes the word "Pecten" is used. According to authorities in such matters, the ears, or wings, on a true Pecten's hings line are about equal in size.

Scallops are superb swimmers, in any direction. They propel themselves by opening and snapping shut their valves, thereby creating jets of water. This jet propulsion is powered by a single strong muscle, which is the only part of the scallop that we eat.

Scallops are found throughout the world in all seas, in deep or shallow water. Like the Pen shell, the lovely scallop also merits a historical footnote. During the Middle Ages, a particular Mediterranean species became a religious symbol and adorned the shields of Crusaders. In England, a scallop on a family's coat of arms indicates that an ancestor was a Crusader.

Long after the Crusades, the British nobility went quite berserk over shells, sometimes going so far as to decorate entire rooms with them. A shell trading company brought specimens to England from all parts of the world. The company branched out a bit and began to sell petroleum oil. When this sideline became extraordinarily profitable, the company stopped bothering with shells. However, the Shell Oil Company still retains the large orange scallop as its trademark, and their tankers bear the names of several families of shells.

Bay Scallop (2 - 3″)

Bay Scallops range from Nova Scotia to Florida. As you might expect, this particular species is divided into three "subspecies." The Bay Scallops that you find on Sanibel and Captiva belong to the subspecies called "Gulf Scallops." In any event, Bay Scallops are the common ones that are dredged along the East Coast, supplying many tons each year for the markets.

Our Gulf Scallop is the plumpest of the three Bay Scallops. The shell may have only 12 - 17 ribs, and the color depends upon which valve you have found. We have found large specimens that are black, dirty white, and orange.

Calico Scallop (1 - 2″)

As is the case with all bivalves, the upper valve of this shell is the more colorful. Calico Scallops derive their name from the great variety of color patterns they display. You can easily find combinations of pink, white, orange, brown, and purple. The shell has about 20 ribs.

Cat's Paw (½ - 1″)

You can always find a Cat's Paw on our Gulf beaches at any time of the year. These small, thick-shelled bivalves have 6 or 7 broad, radial ribs. The basic color is gray, with splashes of brown on the strong, prominent ribs. Shells that have been exposed to the sun for a while quickly lose the brown markings.

Lion's Paw (See Chapter 7)

Rough Scallop (½ - 1½″)

The 18 - 20 ribs on this shell are rather scaly, unless the scales have been worn down by exposure to the elements. Reddish brown and light red are fairly common colors. Collectors are always eager to find a rare lemon-yellow specimen.

UNIVALVES

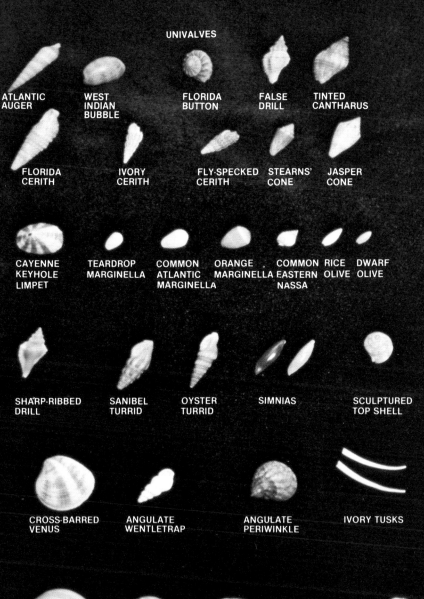

ATLANTIC AUGER

WEST INDIAN BUBBLE

FLORIDA BUTTON

FALSE DRILL

TINTED CANTHARUS

FLORIDA CERITH

IVORY CERITH

FLY-SPECKED CERITH

STEARNS' CONE

JASPER CONE

CAYENNE KEYHOLE LIMPET

TEARDROP MARGINELLA

COMMON ATLANTIC MARGINELLA

ORANGE MARGINELLA

COMMON EASTERN NASSA

RICE OLIVE

DWARF OLIVE

SHARP-RIBBED DRILL

SANIBEL TURRID

OYSTER TURRID

SIMNIAS

SCULPTURED TOP SHELL

CROSS-BARRED VENUS

ANGULATE WENTLETRAP

ANGULATE PERIWINKLE

IVORY TUSKS

COMMON ATLANTIC SLIPPER

SPOTTED SLIPPER

FLAT SLIPPER

CONVEX SLIPPER

THORNY SLIPPER

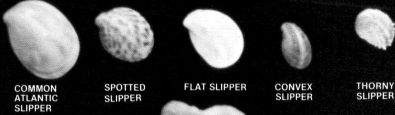

WORM SHELL

UNIVALVES

ALPHABET CONE

FLORIDA CONE

FIGHTING CONCH

FIGHTING CONCH (IMMATURE)

PAPER FIG

KING'S CROWN

CAT'S EYE

SHARK'S EYE

NUTMEG

LETTERED OLIVE

APPLE MUREX

LACE MUREX

BANDED TULIP

TRUE TULIP

PEAR WHELK

LIGHTNING WHELK

HORSE CONCH

BIVALVES

PURPLE
SEMELE

SPINY PAPER
COCKLE

YELLOW
COCKLE

PRICKLY
COCKLE

BROAD-RIBBED
CARDITA

CALICO CLAM

JINGLES

LITTLE
CORRUGATED
JEWEL BOX

SPINY
JEWEL BOX

PURPLE TAGELUS

ROUGH
SCALLOP

CALICO SCALLOP

TULIP MUSSEL

ATLANTIC RIBBED
MUSSEL

CAT'S PAW

IMPERIAL
VENUS

CROSS-BARRED
VENUS

COQUINAS

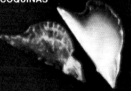

ROSE-PETAL TELLIN

ATLANTIC WING OYSTER

BIVALVES

CUT-RIBBED ARK

MOSSY ARK

PONDEROUS ARK

TRANSVERSE ARK

TURKEY WING

GIANT ATLANTIC COCKLE

BAY SCALLOP

COMMON EGG COCKLE

BUTTERCUP LUC

CHANNELED DUCK CLAM

SUNRAY VENUS

EASTERN OYS

DOSINIA

LIGHTNING VENUS

ALTERNATE TELLIN

ATLANTIC SURF CLAM

QUAHOG

SAW-TOOTHED PEN SHELL

RIGID PEN SHELL

RARE SHELLS

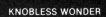

KNOBLESS WONDER

JUNONIA

COMMON SUNDIAL

BABY'S EAR

LION'S PAW

SCOTCH BONNET

ANGEL WING

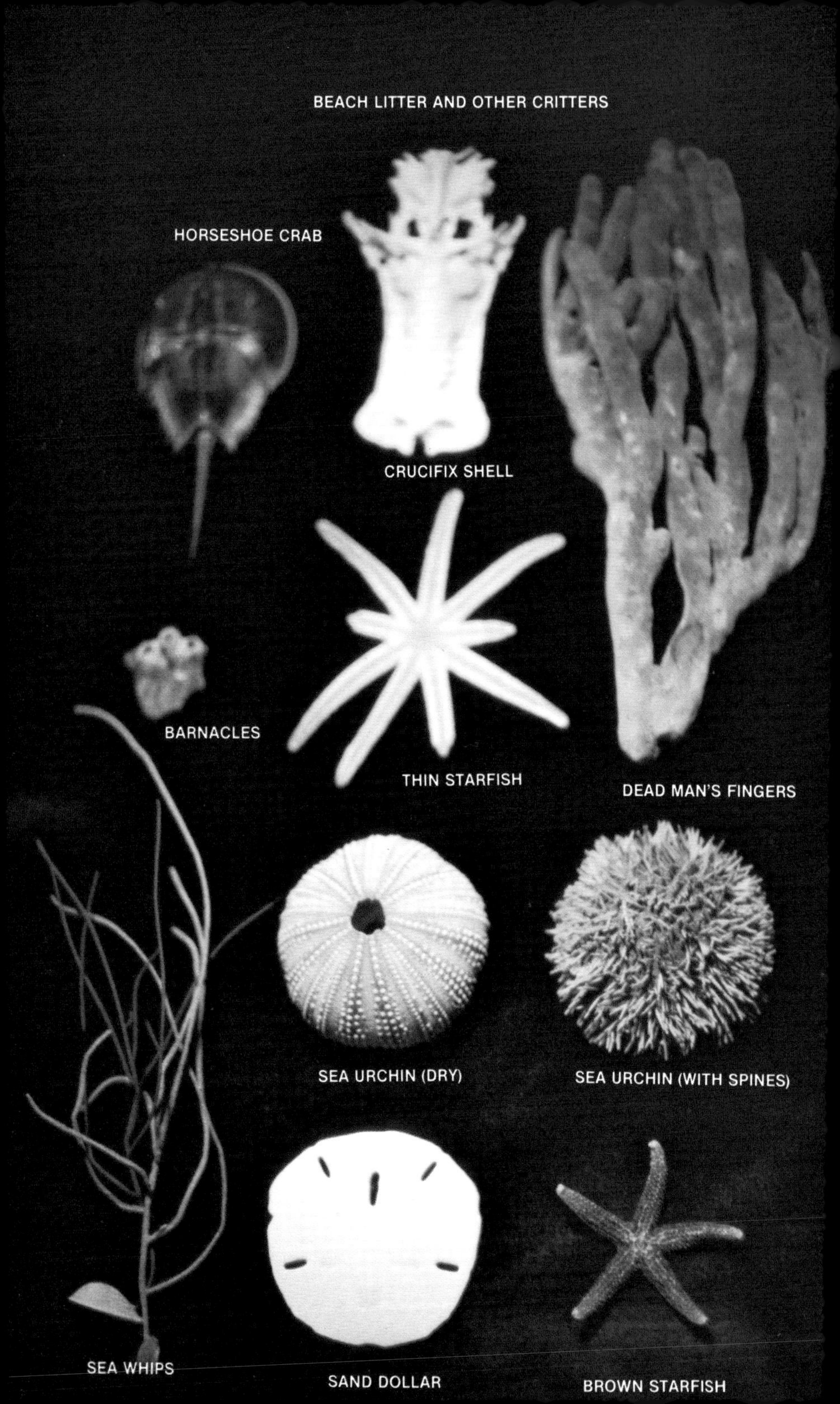

BEACH LITTER AND OTHER CRITTERS

HORSESHOE CRAB

CRUCIFIX SHELL

BARNACLES

THIN STARFISH

DEAD MAN'S FINGERS

SEA URCHIN (DRY)

SEA URCHIN (WITH SPINES)

SEA WHIPS

SAND DOLLAR

BROWN STARFISH

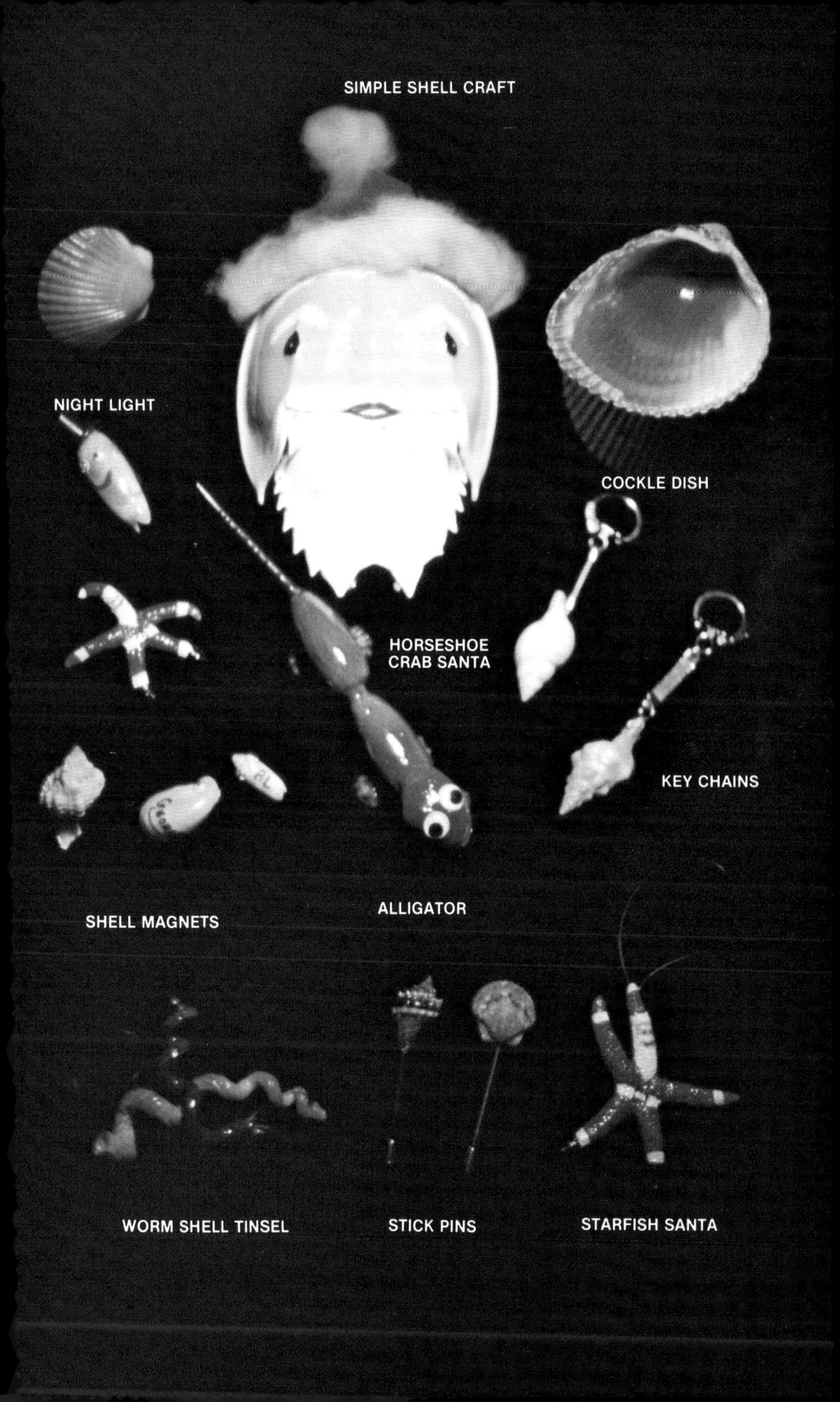

SIMPLE SHELL CRAFT

NIGHT LIGHT

COCKLE DISH

HORSESHOE
CRAB SANTA

KEY CHAINS

SHELL MAGNETS

ALLIGATOR

WORM SHELL TINSEL

STICK PINS

STARFISH SANTA

PRINTER'S TRAY WITH SHELLS

Purple Semele
Orange Semele (1 - 1½ ")

Semeles are quite colorful, thin-shelled clams. They are probably more common in southern Florida than they are here — despite the claim of some detailed texts that several species are common from North Carolina to the Caribbean. The largest American species do appear along the Pacific coast, and these clams are reported to be delicious. The smaller, and more colorful, thin-shelled specimens are used very extensively in shell craft.

When this book was first printed, we had found only one valve of a Purple Semele — and this flawed specimen bore the telltale hole of a carnivorous snail. Subsequently, a lady gave us several of her own lovely samples. All are beautifully marked with a series of pale, wavy purple (or orange) lines.

While seemingly smooth to the touch, there are many extremely fine growth lines. The interior or the shell is glossy white, and the shell is so thin that the markings on the exterior are quite visible when viewed from the interior.

SURF CLAMS

Members of this family are often oval in shape, and are found in abundance throughout the world. You will generally find them on our Gulf beaches at any time.

Atlantic Surf Clam (1 - 6")

The common Atlantic Surf Clam is harvested commercially in North America, especially off the coast of New Jersey. Of course, commercial fishermen do not pick up these clams while strolling on the beach. Instead, they dredge up millions of them every year at depths of up to 80 feet.

You will often find both valves of this sturdy, oval shell washed up intact. The exterior of the smooth shell is basically a creamy tan color. There is generally a darker tan border of coating around the outer edge.

Channeled Duck Clam (1 - 3")

Unlike the Atlantic Surf Clam, the Channeled Duck Clam is almost triangular rather than oval, quite fragile rather than sturdy, and it is highly unusual to find both valves of this clam washed ashore intact during the summer months. What these two clams do have in common, however, is a spoon-like cavity on the hinge line inside.

Known locally as a "Sailor's Ear," the entire shell is pure white in color. The exterior has numerous raised concentric ribs that are very pronounced.

Purple Tagelus (1 - 1½")

The best place to find the delicate Purple Tagelus, or "Corrugated Razor Clam," is on Bay-side mud flats. Members of this family are very partial to brackish water and the muddy areas around mangrove roots.

This lovely, fragile shell is elongate, and the smooth surface is generally quite shiny. The exterior of the shell is purple, marked by very faint purple rays. The interior is frequently a deeper purple.

74

TELLINS

The valves of this large family of clams are generally equal in size, and not very inflated. Some of the most shiny and colorful bivalves belong to this group of mollusks. In some specimens, colorful rays remind one of a beautiful sunrise, or sunset.

Tellins have a large foot that enables them to burrow both quickly and deeply in the sand. We have had good luck in finding Tellins on the Bay side of Sanibel.

Alternate Tellin (2 - 3 ½")

This shell is fairly common on mud flats at low tide. Rather oval in shape, and creamy white or pink in color, the Alternate Tellin is quite shiny. You can easily detect many fine, concentric growth lines.

Rose-Petal Tellin (1 - 1 ½")

Poke around the exposed mud flats off the little Causeway islands at low tide and you will surely find both valves of this lovely shell — at any time of the year. The color of the smooth, glossy shell is either white or pink.

Since these dainty valves resemble rose petals, and the supply is plentiful, the Rose-Petal Tellin is used extensively for making shell flowers.

VENUS CLAMS

The Venus family of clams is well represented on Sanibel throughout the year. A number of these shells show fine sculpture and lovely color. Many edible Venus clams are in great demand by univalves, crabs, shell collectors, shell crafters, and those of us who just love to eat clams.

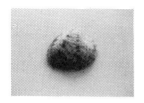

Calico Clam (1 - 3″)

Fairly common throughout the year on our Gulf beaches, the smooth, rather glossy exterior of this sturdy, egg-shaped clam is light beige in color with brown markings. The pattern of these markings causes some shellers to call it a "Checkerboard Clam."

Cross-Barred Venus (½ - 1½″)

This may not be one of the Islands' most exciting specimens. However, it has the virtue of being utterly reliable, and you can find the shell on Gulf beaches at any time of the year.

The small, thick shell derives its name from the presence of many radial ribs that are crossed by concentric ridges of similar size. The grayish white exterior is usually decorated with radiating splashes of brown. The glossy interior is generally purple.

Disk Dosinia and Elegant Dosinia (2 - 3½″)

You can easily find these two clams washed ashore at any time of the year. They are both rather thin, white, circular shells of similar size. You will often find both valves washed up intact. The Disk Dosinia is smoother to the touch, although both specimens are glossy. If you really want to know which one you have found, you will have to take out a magnifying glass and count the concentric ridges. The Elegant Dosinia has 20 - 25 per inch, whereas the Disk Dosinia has about 50, finer ridges per inch.

Imperial Venus (½ - 1½")

This specimen is not found so readily on our beaches as are other Venus clams. While its shape is very typical of the family, the shell is rather unique in one respect: it has 5 - 7 large, concentric ribs that are unusually heavy and rounded. The furrows between these broad ribs are extremely deep. The creamy color of the shell is often marked with brown dots and rays. The high gloss associated with the lovely Imperial Venus may not be present in beach specimens.

Lightning Venus (1 - 2")

This is quite a plump clam shell with many crowded, and extremely prominent, concentric growth lines. The exterior of the shell is white, with splashes of brown arranged in a radial pattern. The interior is polished white, with smooth margins.

Northern and Southern Quahogs (2 - 6")

You can find both kinds of Quahog (pronounced "Co-hog") clams at any time of the year on our beaches. We have had good luck in finding these large, thick, heavy shells on the Gulf beach at North Captiva, and also on the Bay side of Sanibel.

Both Quahogs make excellent ashtrays. However, the Northern Quahog has always had an important commercial value as well. Unlike the Southern Quahog, this clam shell has a deep purple stain in the white interior. The Indians made beads out of this stained area and used them as "wampum," or money.

Smaller Northern Quahogs, known as Littlenecks or Cherrystones (depending upon their size) are extremely important commercially. The Cherrystone is a small Quahog, while the Littleneck is the young off-spring of a Quahog that is large enough to eat raw. In any event, both specimens tend to end up in restaurants.

We have often found a single Quahog shell on the beach with a bluish hue, marked with light brown zigzag lines. This is the prized commercial clam shell. Unfortunately, no amount of oil and lighter fluid seems to preserve either the color or the markings of this shell.

The Southern Quahog almost never has the purple stain on the inside of the shell. Moreover, the clam is of no commercial value since its flavor is considered too strong.

Sunray Venus (2 - 5 ½ ")

It seems fitting to end our discussion of various bivalves with the Sunray Venus, certainly one of our most beautiful shells and a fine addition to any collection. We have had very good luck in finding both valves of this lovely shell on the Bay side of Sanibel and Captiva throughout the year, when the tide is low and the flats are fairly exposed.

The color of this magnificent shell is light purple to gray, with darker radial markings. The exterior is always smooth with a porcelain-like finish. But, should you take a live specimen, you will find that the shiny exterior coating peels off when you boil the shell — and the shell may also turn red.

Unlike many clams, the Sunray Venus is only half-buried in the sand as it feeds. Most other clams really like to burrow in the sand. This makes it relatively easy for shellers to find a fine specimen, but it also makes it very easy for Horse Conchs and Lightning Whelks to enjoy a royal feast! If you feel that you must take a live Sunray Venus, then you should at least enjoy this succulent clam.

CHAPTER 6
THE WORLD OF MINIATURES AND BABY SHELLS

The Shoreline Snooper

THROUGH A MAGNIFYING GLASS

Miniatures are tiny shells that measure no more than half an inch at maturity. We have included a number of the more common specimens in the chapters on univalves and bivalves. Amateur shellers can easily find miniatures at any time of the year on our Islands. If you wish to know more about the fascinating world of these diminutive, exquisitely sculpted shells, then you must buy a magnifying glass, renounce your amateur-sheller status, and consult extremely detailed, authoritative books on the subject.

Many shellers are surpised to learn that miniatures account for about three quarters of all species that have been identified. Therefore, the overwhelming majority of the 400-odd species of shells found on Sanibel and Captiva are miniatures.

True miniature enthusiasts will often fill a bucket with sand and shell scrap. The contents of the bucket are later examined at home, often with the aid of a mangifying glass.

One of the best ways to find miniatures is to sit and sift. All you have to do is sit down by a pile of scrap shells and sift through them. This method of shelling is both rewarding and relaxing.

If you feel somewhat more vigorous, you may want to emulate the Shoreline Snooper. The sharp-eyed Snooper follows the trail of the high-tide line, clutching a plastic baggie filled with tiny treasures.

You can find miniatures just about anywhere, and no time of the year is disappointing. When the tide is out, the area around wharf pilings often yields a good harvest. Should you find pieces of dry seaweed on the beach, give them a good shake. Something interesting may well fall out.

THROUGH A MICROSCOPE

Some miniatures are so minute as to be invisible to the naked eye! This is yet another world of perfectly formed, intricately carved specimens. The search for tiny miniatures is often so rewarding that highly sophisticated shellers may graduate to "microscopics." Avid experts will take home a little pile of sand and examine it carefully under a microscope. Displaying microscopic shells involves quite advanced photographic techniques.

BABY SHELLS

If you are not quite ready for the magnifying glass or the microscope approach to shelling, you may well enjoy building up a collection of baby shells. More properly referred to as "immature" specimens, these little shells are often as small as true miniatures. However, baby shells will be much larger upon maturity. The Horse Conch is, perhaps, the most striking example. In their infancy, bright orange Horse Conchs may be no bigger than miniatures. At full maturity, however, they may be nearly two feet long!

Baby shells often seek refuge in bigger specimens. When the large Pen shells are washed up intact on our beaches, a very common occurrence, look inside a few of them. You will often find that the rather unattractive Pen shell contains a lot of life. You may find baby Jewel Boxes, Murex, Banded Tulips, and perhaps a Simnia. Pen shells are havens for little creatures that are either small by nature, or in the process of growing.

CHAPTER 7
RARE SHELLS

"Oh yoo hoo Juonias, Lions' Paws, Scotch Bonnets!"

Every sheller dreams of finding a rare specimen for his collection. In shelling, one soon learns that nothing is impossible. On Sanibel Island, the odds in favor of amateur shellers are far better than almost anywhere else in the world.

Some people have shelled here for over 20 years and found only one Junonia, or none at all. On the other hand, we know of a woman who found three perfect Junonias in one morning! Moreover, it is not uncommon to read in the local papers that a weekend visitor, or a young child, stumbled upon this prize specimen — even in the summer. (Frankly, we share the skepticism of many Islanders regarding the true origin of summer Junonias — often found conveniently near resorts at a time when there is little more than shell scrap on the Gulf beaches.)

Finding a rare shell is largely a question of luck. It should be comforting to know that you have as good a chance as any expert at being in the right place at the right time.

Two of the shells listed in this chapter, the Baby's Ear and the Angel Wing, are not really that rare. However, one has to know where to look and what to look for. If you wait for these specimens to wash up on the beach, as you must do for rare shells that are not really native to Sanibel, then you are likely to have a very long, lonely, and unrewarding vigil.

Angel Wing (4 - 8″)

The Angel Wing is definitely native to the Islands. Unfortunately, so many of these magnificent bivalve clams have been taken alive, that it is increasingly difficult to find them. Therefore, finding an Angel Wing involves knowing when and where to look for one.

So far as the Gulf side of Sanibel is concerned, we have had good luck in finding Angel Wings during the winter months. The best time to find these delicate pure-white shells is during a particularly low tide. The shell will usually be partially buried in the sand, but quite visible. However, you will not normally find both valves of this shell on the Gulf side.

If you must have both valves for your collection, then your best bet is to scour the muddy flats near mangroves on the Bay side. At this point, you may decide that beauty ends where hard work begins!

One of the most powerful of the boring clams, the edible Angel Wing loves to burrow in mud and muck where it thrives one foot (or more) below the surface. Be prepared to wallow around in knee-deep mud that is loaded with sharp, broken pieces of shells. Be prepared to have a sneaker pulled off when attempting to walk in the quagmire. When you see a siphon protruding from the burrow, start digging at an angle. If you dig right over the siphon, you are likely to break the shell. Once you have located your prize (assuming that the siphon belonged to an Angel Wing) be very gentle in removing it. Since the Angel Wing is quite delicate, it can easily break as you loosen it from the suction of the mud. Now, of course, you must clean your specimen. Most shellers feel that the addition of a flawless specimen to their collections is well worth the considerable effort involved.

The Angel Wing is perfectly named, so there is no problem at all in identifying what you have found. The snowy-white shell is thin and quite fragile. There are some 26 radial ribs, with little scales, that are very well defined. A specimen with pink stains inside the shell is a particularly rare find.

Baby's Ear (½ - 1½")

The Baby's Ear is one of the Moon Snails (See Chapter 4). Like the Angel Wing, this specimen is native to Sanibel and not really that rare. Once again, however, one has to know where to look and what to look for. It is highly unlikely that an incoming tide will send a Baby's Ear rolling up to your feet, in which case you might not see it anyway.

Your best hunting ground is an exposed sand bar on the Gulf side at low tide. Like its relatives, this snail likes to burrow in the sand. A friend of ours pokes around the sand bar with an ice cream scoop. She looks for what she calls a "plop" (a little mound) and digs under it. What she uncovers looks like a glob of dark, wet sand that is all stuck together. Actually, this is the mantle of the snail, covered with sand. The shell itself is not visible until you boil the "plop" in water for about one minute. Only then can you detach the Baby's Ear shell.

Like the Angel Wing, the Baby's Ear is well named — although most mothers would have cause for concern if an infant's ear were that small! This round, milky-white shell may be no more than 1½ inches in diameter, and no more than half an inch high. There are 3 or 4 whorls, and the opening is quite large.

Common Sundial (1 - 2″)

Although one of the Island's largest resorts bears the name of this shell, there is nothing at all "common" about it in our part of the world. We mention this specimen only because so many books indicate that you may find one here. We have seen a few Sundials in other people's collections, and they were not very colorful specimens. If you would like a Sundial for your collection, our local shell shops will not disappoint you.

Like the Baby's Ear, the Common Sundial is circular and flat. It may be 1½ inches in diameter and about ¾ of an inch high. A most attractive specimen, the Sundial has 6 or 7 whorls and several beaded, spiral cords. The basic color is grayish white or tan, spotted with brown and purple.

Junonia (3 - 6″)

This valuable, highly prized "volute" is not really native to the Islands, for the mollusk lives at depths of up to 200 feet. However, a number are washed ashore on our Gulf beaches every year, especially during the winter months. You stand just as good a chance of finding one as anyone else. It is just a matter of luck.

In their natural habitat, some distance from shore and at considerable depth, the Junonia is not that rare. Shrimp fishermen haul them in quite regularly, a circumstance that may explain why our local shell shops are well stocked with fine specimens. Some Sanibel residents have found Junonias in their driveways. Others paw through mounds of displaced sand at construction sites, or haunt dredging sites.

This univalve is a spiral-shaped shell with about 5 whorls. The color is creamy white, with numerous rows of orange to brown, squarish spots. Should you be so fortunate as to find a Junonia, identification will not be a problem!

Knobless Wonder (up to 18″)

Also known as the "Bumpless Wonder," this rare specimen is not a deformed Horse Conch without bumps. It is a different variety of Horse Conch that never attains quite the size if its "gigantea" relative.

Another pecularity of this specimen is that it makes its rare appearance only around Sanibel and Captiva and, even more rarely, southward as far as Marco Island. The lovely shell that appears in color was found on the Bay side of our Islands.

Lion's Paw (2 - 6″)

If the Junonia is a shell collector's dream, then the Lion's Paw ranks with the Holy Grail. Like the Junonia, this magnificent bivalve scallop is not really native to the Islands. It thrives some distance beyond our shores in depths of up to 100 feet. After a strong storm, someone might find a single valve of this scallop washed up on a Gulf beach.

We have found only broken pieces. It appears that sponge fishermen stand the best chance of finding a Lion's Paw.

The shell of this beautiful specimen is rather heavy and quite sturdy. There are 7-9 strong ribs, which are marked with smaller "riblets" and bumps. The exterior color reminds one of red wine. Orange and yellow specimens are extremely rare.

Scotch Bonnet (2 - 4″)

This attractive univalve has a penchant for Sea Urchins and Sand Dollars. Therefore, the mollusk thrives on a sandy bottom in fairly shallow water. Occasionally, a good storm will wash the Scotch Bonnet ashore. Once again, finding one is all a question of luck. Shellers in the Florida Keys often have more luck in finding a Scotch Bonnet than shellers in the "shell capital of the world."

The Scotch Bonnet is quite a sturdy shell with about 5 whorls and a short, pointed tip. The curved outer lip is thick, and the opening is quite large. The basic creamy color of the exterior is artfully decorated with rather square, light-brown spots.

CHAPTER 8

BEACH LITTER
AND OTHER CRITTERS

Detritus Touristorum Americanorum

The City of Sanibel hopes that its residents and visitors will leave only their footprints in the sand. Should you find samples of Detritus Touristorum Americanorum on our beaches, there is absolutely no restriction on the number of specimens you may pick up and throw into the nearest trash bin. UNLIMITED SPECIMENS PER SPECIES PER PERSON!

OTHER FOOTPRINTS: ECHINODERMS

Mollusks are by no means the only interesting specimens that you will encounter as you wade in the Gulf or walk on the beaches. There is quite a variety of animal life that many people enjoy watching, and sometimes collecting for decorative purposes or for use in shell craft.

Echinoderms are especially popular specimens. These are marine animals that have limy plates, frequently with spines, that serve as "skeletons." In some Starfish, these plates are connected at movable joints. Or, in the case of Sea Urchins, they form a continuous shell. Sometimes, the plates are not connected at all, as is the case with Sea Cucumbers.

In any event, adult Echinoderms all exhibit a star-like pattern. In some cases, radiating arms are equipped with tube feet that help the animal get a good grip on surfaces as it tries to move and obtain food.

Sand Dollar (up to 5 ″)

The Sand Dollar, also called a "Keyhole Urchin," belongs to the Urchin family. This flat, round disc has 5 slots and, when alive, is covered with short, greenish-brown spines. Half-buried in the sand, the animal feeds on plankton and organic material, warding off enemies by secreting a smelly, yellow fluid.

The best place to look for Sand Dollars is on exposed sand bars, for they rarely make it to shore in one piece. Live specimens will need a good bath in Clorox for 24 hours, followed by a period in the sun to bleach them out.

The Sand Dollar, like the Crucifix Shell, is associated with religious symbolism. It is sometimes referred to as the "Holy Ghost Shell," and various Christmas and Easter symbols have been noted. The design on one side of this disc is thought to resemble the Easter lily, while that on the other side represents the poinsettia. According to the popular legend, the 5 holes represent the wounds Christ received from nails and a Roman sword. The teeth of the Sand Dollar, located in the center, are thought to resemble little white doves of peace.

Sea Urchin (up to 3 ")

The spiny Sea Urchin is another inhabitant of sand bars and flats. The limy plates of Sea Urchins, like those of Sand Dollars, are joined to form a shell. They also exhibit a five-rayed pattern of pores for the suction-cupped tubular feet, which shows their close relationship to Starfish.

Live Sea Urchins are covered with spines, deep rose in color. We have seen these fragile shells used for everything from shell-craft toadstools to night lights and small lamp shades.

Starfish

Starfish are yet another one of the Echinoderms that leave a distinctive trail on the flats, or on Gulf-side sand. These animals love to feast on clams and, most especially, oysters. Starfish have the dubious distinction of being responsible for destroying millions of dollars worth of shellfish every year.

In discussing the trials and tribulations of oysters in Chapter 5, we noted that the starfish is an extraordinarily patient predator. It will wrap all its arms (rays) around a hapless oyster and pull very steadily — for several hours, if necessary. When the oyster's exhausted muscles begin to relax a bit, causing the valves to part, the starfish enjoys a succulent meal in quite a singular manner. It actually extends its stomach through its mouth into the oyster, which it digests then and there. Once sated, the starfish throws away whatever it considers to be trash, and retracts its stomach. This terror of the oyster beds has been known to breed in great numbers, and completely consume a large bed of oysters.

Brown Starfish (up to 3″)

This specimen is very common around Sanibel and Captiva. It usually has 5 arms (4 or 6 being quite uncommon), with sucking discs that aid in movement and in latching on to Sea Urchins and bivalves. Many Florida starfish are called "Breaking Stars," for they have the annoying habit of dropping off an arm when captured. (They subsequently grow a replacement arm, but it is not normally so long as the original.)

Thin Starfish (up to 16″)

This specimen is somewhat less common than the Brown Starfish. Generally beige or gray in color, the "Nine-Arm Starfish" often leaves its outline in the sand above it. A depression is created when the buried starfish takes in and expels water, blowing away the sand above in the process.

OTHER TRAILS: CRUSTACEANS

Marine anthropods are almost entirely crustaceans, of which there are some 25,000 species. Marine crustaceans range in size from nearly microscopic forms to veritable Goliaths with legs that are five feet long! Some crustaceans, like lobsters, certain crabs, and shrimp, have considerable commercial value. Smaller crustaceans serve as food for other marine life.

All crustaceans have an external skeleton and segmented bodies. As the animal grows, it sheds its old skeleton and grows a new one. During the period between skeletons, however, the animal tries to hide as much as possible, for it is extremely vulnerable.

Barnacles

Anyone who has owned a boat knows what a nuisance barnacles can be. These creatures attach themselves to rocks, wood, cement pilings, or whatever else is available.

Barnacles do not look or behave very much like other crustaceans. Free-swimming larvae change in form as they grow. Attaching themselves to rocks, etc., the larvae rest for a time and then become adults with shells that have overlapping divisions. Barnacles come equipped with feathery feet that brush plankton into the mouth of the animal. Shellers are often dismayed by the barnacle's seeming propensity to latch on to especially fine shell specimens!

Crabs

If you do any wading on either side of our Islands, you are bound to encounter several kinds of crabs. While some appear to be ferocious and ready to do battle with your big toe, try to remember that these creatures are only afraid that you want to do unto them what you fear that they may want to do unto you. Probably both of you will back off, and that will be the end of the close encounter of the fourth kind.

Fiddler Crab

This brownish crab likes to burrow in sandy beaches. In walking along the short, sandy path that leads from the Bay side of North Captiva to the Gulf, we were quite startled by the rattling noise of hundreds of these harmless Fiddler Crabs. It seemed as though a horde of locusts had descended upon this peaceful isle. Actually, countless Fiddler Crabs were merely scurrying about — sideways.

The little Fiddler Crab derives its name from the fact that one of the male's two claws is very large. This claw is not normally used against human beings. In fact, it is rarely used at all, other than in fierce mating-season battles.

Hermit Crab

This creature is a great freeloader, and you are very likely to encounter him living in another animals's shell. Hermit Crabs live rent-free out of necessity, for they produce no shells of their own. These crabs use only empty shells, the size of their temporary home depending upon the size of the growing crab. Tiny Hermit Crabs will steal miniature shells, while hideous, red, giant monsters may glare at you from the opening of a very large Horse Conch.

Swimming Crabs

These crabs are apt to put up a ferocious false front as you wade by. They belong to a family in which the last pair of legs is rather flattened, and thus well adapted for swimming.

Blue Crab (about 6″)

These are the crabs that we like to eat. They are extremely plentiful on the Bay side of our Islands, since they prefer brackish water. Like other crustaceans, the young crabs shed their shells as they grow, reaching maturity in about one year. Crabs caught soon after molting are sold as "soft-shelled" crabs. However, there is no difference between these specimens and the "hard-shelled" Blue Crabs.

Calico Crab (about 3″)

The Calico, or "Lady" Crab, has a speckled pattern on its light-brown shell. Its hind legs are not so well adapted for swimming as are those of the Blue Crab, and it prefers sandy areas.

Horseshoe Crab:
A Living Fossil (up to 20″)

The Horseshoe Crab is a living fossil whose ancestors, which it closely resembles, go back to Cambrian times some 500 million years ago. One of the world's oldest forms of animal life, this specimen is gradually disappearing, due to its frequent use in fertilizers.

The Horseshoe Crab is not a crab, and not a crustacean. Rather, it is a marine relative of spiders and scorpions. Like crustaceans, however, the Horseshoe Crab discards its shell as it grows. You will frequently find these tan, horny shells washed up on the beach. Older Horseshoe Crabs have much darker shells, and the live animal is sometimes stranded on the beach. Pick up a live crab by the tail and set it on the beach. It will immediately begin the slow, laborious process of turning around and heading back to the water.

Horseshoe Crabs live on the ocean's floor, where their tails leave a trail in the sand. They have 5 pairs of legs, and swim by flapping their gill plates. The life of this ancient creature is very quiet. It does not stray very far from where it started as an adult, and it feeds on marine worms, dead fish and other organic matter — habits that make them valuable scavengers.

Octopus

During the winter months, it is not uncommon to find small octopuses in shallow water on the Gulf side of the Islands. Sometimes, a receding tide leaves them stranded near a sand bar.

Like all the univalves and bivalves discussed in Chapters 4 and 5, the octopus is a true mollusk — not a crustacean. In fact, it belongs to the highest class of mollusks. This is because an octopus has a brain, 3 hearts, blue blood, 2 kidneys, perfect eyes — but no outside shell.

Millions of years ago, this creature reigned supreme in the oceans. Even now, the octopus should always be taken very seriously. The arms of Atlantic specimens may be three feet long, while the largest Pacific variety may weigh over 100 pounds.

An octopus moves by swimming along with squid-like jet propulsion, its 8 arms dangling behind. Or, it may crawl along the bottom, stopping to envelop a victim in its rubbery, suction-cupped arms. The creature finds crabs, and many kinds of live meat, extremely appealing. An octopus will bite its victim, and then suck it in alive.

When you see young octopuses stranded near the shore, remember that even these small specimens have sharp teeth that can give a nasty bite to the hand that reaches out to pick them up, with the hope of getting them into a jar of formaldehyde.

Crucifix Shell

This is not a shell by any definition. Rather, it is the headbone of a sail catfish. Since the Crucifix Shell is supposed to bring the finder good luck, you may wish to look for one on Bay-side mud flats. Fishermen generally throw back catfish in disgust, and the skeletal headbone is the only part of this fish that other sea creatures do not find at all appetizing. Therefore, you stand a very good chance of finding this token of good luck.

A legend concerning the crucifixion of Christ is associated with this bone. According to the legend, God is reminding us of Christ's suffering. One sees in the bone structure the outline of Jesus on the Cross, and the wound in his side where the sword was plunged. The rattling produced when one shakes this bone is meant to portray the sound of dice as they tossed for Christ's robes.

SPONGES

Many kinds of sponges, or parts of sponges, are washed up on our Gulf beaches. For example, you may find pieces of "Bath Sponges." These are the specimens that divers gather up. Once dried, bleached, and cleaned, they may be sold. Tarpon Springs, Florida, is still the center for American sponge fishing. However, the introduction of artificial sponges has caused this industry to suffer considerably.

Dead Man's Fingers

Commonly washed ashore on our Gulf beaches, this reddish-orange specimen is not a "Bath" sponge but a "Horny" sponge. Many beachcombers like to pick up this kind of sponge, and others, as a souvenir or as a prop for displaying shells.

Just remember that all sponges have to be thoroughly dried out in order to preserve them. This process is best accomplished far away from everything and everyone, for sponges emit an utterly foul stench while curing. Once it has been dried out, this particular specimen turns grayish-brown.

UNWELCOME VISITORS

During the summer months, and even well into the fall, shellers need to watch out for two most unwelcome creatures: Jellyfish and Stingrays.

Moon Jellyfish (3 - 9")

The Moon Jellyfish is extremely common in the waters around our Islands. This milky disc, with very short tentacles, is often washed up on the beach. When wading during warm weather, one should always keep an eye out for these creatures. Their sting, a prickling irritation that may cause a rash, can be rather unpleasant.

Stingray

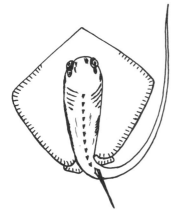

Stingrays are also particularly abundant during the warm summer months. Their favorite habitats are the shallow waters on either the Gulf or the Bay side of our Islands. They generally lie on top of the sand, or somewhat buried in it, and their tan or light-brown color makes it very difficult to distinguish them from the environment into which they blend so well.

At times, entire squadrons of stingrays will swim within inches of the shore, and it is miraculous that they avoid being washed up onto the beach. It certainly would be wise to avoid swimming or shelling when stingrays are out in such force.

The ''Sanibel Shuffle'' that we described at the end of Chapter 3 is designed to let stingrays know that you are approaching. Theoretically, they do not care to meet you any more than you care to meet them.

However, there is occasionally a most unpleasant encounter between an absorbed sheller and a preoccupied stingray.

The weight of your foot on a stingray causes the animal to fling up its barbed tail and penetrate your flesh. The barb goes in easily enough, but removing it is quite another matter for the edges of the arrow-like barb are serrated. Moreover, a damaged barb releases venom into the wound. The intense pain caused by the puncture may be accompanied by vomiting, diarrhea, and even muscular paralysis. Anyone who experiences such an unpleasant encounter with a stingray should seek medical attention immediately.

SEA WHIPS

While the Sea Whip resembles a plant, it is actually a coral growth. Both yellow and reddish-purple Sea Whips are frequently washed ashore on our Gulf beaches, and they are used extensively as background props in shell craft.

You will often find several kinds of shells attached to Sea Whips. Although you may not be the least bit interested in adding yet another Ponderous Ark to your collection, you will certainly want to examine Sea Whips very carefully in order to find the glossy little Simnia shells (See Chapter 4.)

SEA OATS

Sea Oats are a common plant on our Gulf shores. They play an extremely important role in preventing erosion on coastal beaches, where their roots help to anchor shifting sand.

The plant derives its name from its strong resemblance to domestic wheat. **A SPECIFIC SECTION IN THE FLORIDA STATUTES STRICTLY PROHIBITS THE REMOVAL OF SEA OATS.**

CHAPTER 9

CLEANING SHELLS

(Expletives Deleted)

GREEDY GUS

Most shellers are aware of Sanibel's live-shelling restriction: two live specimens per species per person. However, there are always a few individuals who seem to go berserk when they hit our beaches. Greedy Gus is a case in point.

Greedy Gus gathers live specimens with gay abandon, utterly oblivious to any sensible restrictions. In fact, his boundless enthusiasm recognizes no limits at all — until his own body betrays him and refuses to bend over any more. If Greedy Gus is not concerned with conservation, we hope that he may be deterred by the thought of cleaning all his illicit loot!

Cleaning shells is not one of the many joys associated with collecting them. Since this book is for amateur shellers, we will discuss general cleaning methods that we have found to be effective. Those who wish to exhibit or display their collections in shell shows, however, will want to consult books that are entirely devoted to this subject.

UNOCCUPIED SHELLS

Most of the shells that you find at the edge of the water, or on the beach, are not live specimens. However, they still require a certain amount of cleaning — especially the univalves.

Rinse the shells thoroughly in water to remove sand, mud, algae, etc. An outdoor faucet is best for this purpose, in order to avoid clogging up the kitchen sink or the disposal. Place the shells on newspaper to dry. Do not be tempted to hasten the drying process by exposing your shells to the sun. While the sun gives some sort of color to human beings, it bleaches all the color out of shells in no time at all.

Once the shells are dry, shake them a bit to dislodge sand — and there always seems to be sand in the nooks and crannies of univalves, no matter how carefully you have cleaned them.

Shells that you find in the mud on the Bay side of the Islands will need more attention. We soak these shells overnight in a weak solution of Clorox and water: 1 cup of Clorox to 1 gallon of water. This process will enable you to remove the slime by using a fairly stiff brush. Chip off barnacles with a nut pick, screw driver, or whatever tool is handy and effective.

Once shells are clean and dry, you may want to coat them in order to bring out their natural color. Nothing, of course, will restore color to shells that have been lying in the sun for any length of time. However, any color that remains can be revived to a considerable degree. For craft purposes, we suggest a clear, crystal spray. Such sprays are readily available at Island shell shops.

Many collectors do not favor sprays at all. In fact, sprayed specimens (other than those used in shell craft) are not acceptable for displays at shell shows or for trade among serious collectors. In order to revive a shell's natural color, we recommend the following solution: 1 part mineral oil to 7 parts lighter fluid. We have experimented with other oils, but find that some leave odors that are not pleasant, while others may attract little creatures that are not welcome additions to your collection.

Take an old toothbrush and apply this solution to the shells. Let the shells stand overnight, and remove excess oil in the morning with a paper towel. The results are always gratifying, and often very surprising as well.

SHELLS WITH OWNERS IN RESIDENCE

Live univalves will have stubborn snails in residence. You would have to be endowed with Herculean strength to pull a snail out of its home, and the outcome of such a struggle would be highly debatable. Bivalves present far less difficulty. However, one has to be extremely careful to avoid breaking the hinge that attaches the two valves. Serious collectors will want to consult more detailed texts on the subject of cleaning bivalves.

Boiling is clearly the fastest and easiest method of removing mollusks from their shells. In choosing a pot, think about the chore of cleaning it later on. We prefer stainless steel or enamel pots. Also, make sure that the pot is large enough to accommodate the shells. You will not want to have dirty foam boiling all over the stove.

Cover the shells with cool water and bring the brew to a boil. Lower the heat so that the water will boil gently, as opposed to vigorously. The length of boiling time depends entirely upon the size of the shells. Two or three minutes are generally enough for most shells. If you have a large Whelk or Horse Conch, however, it might take 20 minutes — or even longer.

Bivalves are done soon after the valves gape open. The best test for univalve snails is to try to remove the door (operculum). If it comes off easily, the snail has boiled long enough. Be sure to clean and set aside the operculum.

Allow the shells to cool until you can handle them. However, it is definitely not a good idea to allow cooked shells to become too cool. Not only will they begin to smell, but the cooled animal will harden and become difficult to remove from the shell.

Bivalve mollusks are easy to remove. Just scoop them out and use a knife to scrape the place where the muscle was attached. To remove univalve snails, however, you will need an instrument. We use a nut pick, a piece of wire, a pin, or the end of a paper clip — depending upon the size of the snail. Pierce the body and give a steady, twisting pull. Most of the time, the entire body will come out in one piece.

Unfortunately, there are times when the body breaks at the soft connections. When this occurs, place the shell in water in order to loosen the remains. You can also try to hold the shell under a running faucet, in the hope that a steady, forceful stream of water will dislodge remaining particles. Another possibility is to slosh the shell around vigorously in a sink full of water. Particles may be dislodged in this manner. As a last resort, we bury shells in dirt under the porch. Cooperative ants invariably succeed in disposing of the deceased.

If you resort to the ant treatment, be sure to bury the shell. Exposure to the sun will ruin the color. This particular method is also very effective for "suspect" shells. After removing the animal from any shell, you should always give the specimen a good sniff before coating it with oil or spraying it. You may often think that the animal came out in one piece, but the sniff test may indicate that you were quite mistaken. The tiniest particle of a dead animal can let off a perfectly dreadful stench. Therefore, if a specimen is at all suspect, let the ants take care of it for you.

Clean, dry shells are now ready to be sprayed, or coated with the oil solution. A number of specimens, like Olives, Cats' Eyes, etc., may require no coating at all since they are naturally rather glossy.

The final step in preparing a univalve for your collection is to replace the operculum, which should be clean and dry. Stuff the shells with cotton. Then, put some glue on the inside of the operculum so that it will adhere to the cotton. Try to replace the operculum in such a manner that the specimen appears to be alive. All professional collectors insist on having the operculum in place.

SHELLS WITH UNINVITED GUESTS

Univalve shells are not always occupied by their snail creators. A small claw, little legs, and beady eyes indicate that a Hermit Crab has taken up residence. You will frequently find Hermit Crabs in very small univalve shells, whose owners met with an untimely death. The smaller the creature, the more fragile and breakable the body. Therefore, special care must be exercised in removing Hermit Crabs.

Shells occupied by these crabs should never be boiled. Hot water causes the creature to retreat into the shell to such a degree that only the ants can get rid of it.

The easiest way to remove a Hermit Crab is to place the shell in cool water. Now add warmer water — but never so hot as to cause the crab to retreat into the shell. Soon, the Hermit Crab will crawl out. We usually let these shells soak in water for several hours. If the crab has not left his shell, at least he is dead and thus relatively easy to remove. Should the body not come out intact, then treat the specimen as you would any other suspect shell. Clean, dry shells are now ready for glaze or oil.

CHAPTER 10

SOME SIMPLE SHELL CRAFT

"Even I can do it!"

A LITTLE IMAGINATION

The only limit to what one creates is one's own imagination. When you browse in our local shell shops, you may well reach the conclusion that the human imagination knows no limits at all!

We are acquainted with one Sanibel resident whose highly original shell-craft creations consistently win the most coveted awards at the annual Shell Show. This remarkable lady has been known to pick up dead fish on the beach, for the sole purpose of extracting particular bones for her floral creations.

Not all of us, however, are blessed with a prize-winning imagination. Therefore, we have devoted this chapter to some very simple articles that anyone can make with local shells, very few materials, and minimal expense.

SPRAY AND GLUE

A good craft spray is essential in order to bring out the color in your shells and give them a nice, glossy finish. Such sprays are readily available in local shell shops. We prefer Crystal Clear Glaze.

Glue is the other essential item for shell craft. The type of glue that you use depends upon what you are making. For an extra strong bond, we recommend an epoxy or instant glue. For most craft projects, however, any glue that dries clear and has a good bond is quite acceptable. In this connection, we recommend Bond 527 for it has a very strong, long-lasting bond and dries clear in a short time.

If you are gluing shells onto styrofoam, or onto flat objects (for a wreath, etc.) we recommend a white glue. Elmer's glue is particularly satisfactory, for it has a strong bond and dries clear.

SHELL MAGNETS

This is one of the easiest objects to make. Shell magnets will enhance the appearance of any refrigerator, and they are lovely, very inexpensive gifts for family and friends.

Equipment: Clean shell of your choice
Magnet
Glue and craft spray

Spray the shell with craft spray and set aside to dry. Once dry, turn the shell over and spray the back. When the shell is thoroughly dry, glue the magnet in place. You will want to position the magnet with an eye to displaying the shell to its best advantage. For shell magnets, we use an epoxy or instant glue to ensure a strong bond.

To lend a personal touch to the shell magnet, you can add eyes, a small plastic hat, and your friend's name to shells like Olives.

SHELL CRITTERS

All kinds of creatures can be made from shells. Just let your imagination run wild!

Alligator

Equipment:
    2 large "headless" Olive shells
    4 Cats' Paws (or Carditas, or small
       Arks)
    1 pair of eyes
    1 Horseshoe Crab tail
    1 piece of wire
    2 Surf clam shells (or Tellin
       shells)
    Glue and craft spray

You can easily find all of the shells listed above at any time of the year on our beaches. Large "headless" Olives (the apex is missing) are commonly discarded by other shellers as imperfect specimens.

Put plenty of glue (Bond 527) on the wire and push it through the two Olives. Let this set until dry. Glue the 2 pairs of Cats' Paws (or small Arks or Carditas) together for the alligator's feet. When dry, glue one pair onto the first Olive, and the other pair onto the second Olive. (Actually, it is best to set the Olives onto the pairs of "feet.") Now glue one of the Surf clams (or Tellins) onto the top of the first Olive, and the other under the first Olive so that the alligator's mouth appears to be open. The tail may be either an extension of the wire, or a Horseshoe Crab's tail glued into the end of the second Olive.

After everything has dried, you may want to paint the body green, and the mouth red. When dry, spray the critter with craft spray. When that is dry, glue on the eyes. Your ferocious alligator is now ready to do battle!

Bird

Equipment:
- 2 Ponderous Ark shells (or Turkey Wings)
- 1 Cat's Eye (or Shark's Eye)
- 1 piece of driftwood
- 2 Coquina shells
- Glue and craft spray

Glue together the two Ark (or Turkey Wing) shells with Bond 527. Slip a rubber band around them until dry. Now glue the Cat's Eye (or Shark's Eye) onto the flat, thicker part of the shell so that it will resemble a bird's head with an eye. Glue the Coquinas into position for the beak. Spray with craft spray and, when dry, glue the bird onto a piece of driftwood.

KEY CHAIN

Key chains, like shell magnets, make very practical, inexpensive gifts for family and friends. In selecting shells for this purpose, we recommend fairly sturdy specimens. If the key chain is for a man, you might also want to avoid shells that have sharp points — conceivably an unpleasant reminder of your devotion when thrust into a pocket.

Equipment: Shell of your choice (Tulip, Olive, Nutmeg, Murex, etc.)
Key chain
Jewelry fixing (not necessary if you drill a hole)
Glue and craft spray

Spray the shell and set it aside to dry. Then glue (epoxy or instant) on a jewelry fixing that has a hole for attaching the key chain. When dry, attach the small ring of a key chain to the jewelry fixing.

Those who like to drill holes can avoid the jewelry fixing entirely. Just remember that the shell should be very sturdy (a Murex or Nutmeg, for example) and one must drill very carefully.

COCKLE SERVING DISHES

It is not hard to find double Cockles at most times of the year on our Islands. The valves of the Giant Atlantic Cockle make ideal dishes for serving condiments, nuts, candy, hors d'oeuvres, etc. Smaller valves can be used for coins, paper clips, pins, and a host of other items that one would prefer not to have cluttering up drawers and desks.

Single Cockle Dish

Equipment:
    2 Cockle valves of equal size
    Glue and craft spray

    Spray both valves with craft spray inside and out. When dry, place one valve face down and glue the other valve onto it (face up).

Double Cockle Dish

Equipment:
    3 Cockle valves of equal size
    Glue and craft spray

    Spray all the valves on both sides and set aside to dry. Now place two valves together, face down, with the narrower ends touching as much as possible. Glue together where they touch with an epoxy glue. (Place the shells on foil before gluing in case the glue spills a bit). When that is dry, balance the third Cockle valve (face up) between the two glued valves (still face down) and glue it onto these valves. When dry, turn the creation over.

All-Purpose Cockle Dish

Equipment:
  5 Cockle valves of equal size
  A shell of your choice for a handle
    (Tulip, Alphabet Cone, Whelk,
    etc.)
  Glue and craft spray

Spray all Cockle valves inside and out. When dry, place 4 of the valves face down with the narrower ends meeting at the middle. Glue (epoxy) together where the shells meet. When these are dry, turn the dish over and glue the sprayed shell of your choice onto the middle of the 4 valves for a handle.

STICK PIN AND COCKTAIL SWIZZLE STICK

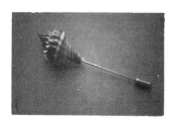

Equipment: Small shell of your choice
           Stick pin (or swizzle stick)
           Glue and craft spray

Spray the shell on both sides and set aside to dry. Glue stick pin (or swizzle stick) on the back of the shell. (Actually, it is very desirable to glue the pin, or stick, into the aperture of the shell.) A strong-bond glue is highly recommended.

CHRISTMAS DECORATIONS

For Christmas decorations, you can really give your imagination free reign. One year, our tree was decorated entirely with shells and starfish Santas. You can string up rows of "headless" Olives to wrap around the tree, and place small Paper Fig shells over colored lights.

108

Worm Shell Tinsel

Equipment: 1 long, curly Worm shell
Clear fishing line
Paint
Glue and craft spray

You can make a Worm shell tinsel simply by spraying the shell with craft spray. Or, if you feel more energetic, paint the shell a bright red, blue, or silver. (If you decide to paint the shell, spray it with craft spray after the paint has dried.) Make a loop out of some clear fishing line, and glue both the ends into the hole of the Worm shell. The finished product is now ready to hang on a tree branch.

Christmas Wreath

Equipment: Circular frame
Many shells
Glue and craft spray

Inexpensive, circular frames of all sizes are readily available in local shell shops, and they will generally have a hanger already attached to the back. You can easily make your own circular frame by sawing one out of plywood or pressboard.

If you choose to make your own frame, you will have to glue (epoxy) or nail a hanger onto the back. For this purpose, you will need small nails and a piece of wood.

Some people like to paint both the inner and outer edges of the frame a bright blue or green, in case the shells do not cover every space. Others place flat shells (such as Coquinas, Tellins, Scallops, etc.) around the inner and outer rims of the frame. Just fill in the center of the frame with the shells of your choice — with or without a pattern.

A white glue is most effective for this kind of work. You can always glue shells on top of other shells, to cover up spaces. When the wreath is finished, spray the shells with craft spray to bring out the colors. Once dry, your creation is ready to hang on your door — perhaps with a nice red bow or some mistletoe.

Starfish Santa

Equipment: One 2-3″ starfish
Paint (red, white, black,
and flesh color)
Glue and craft spray

You can find starfish on Gulf beaches, or on the Bay side of the Islands, throughout the year. Dry these specimens out thoroughly in the sun. Once the starfish is dry, we use a quick-drying, water-base paint. Paint the white part of the Santa first, for this will give you a definite pattern to follow. Pick up the arm you want to use for the head and paint the tip white. A little further down this arm, paint a white ridge for the edge of Santa's hat. Further down this same arm, paint a white beard.

Now paint a white trim for the edge of Santa's red suit on each of the other arms, and a white band in the center for his belt. When dry, turn the starfish over and continue the white on the back. Next paint the face a flesh color and, while that is drying, paint the boots black. Once dry, paint all the other areas red — holding on to the black boots. When dry, continue these colors on the back.

Using a fine brush, paint a red mouth, black eyes, and give Santa a white moustache and white eyebrows. If necessary, touch up all the white areas. Once dry, paint a black buckle on the white belt. When thoroughly dry, spray Santa with craft spray.

The finished starfish Santa can now be made into a magnet, a stick pin, a swizzle stick, or a tree decoration (see previous directions for the first three). For a tree decoration, make a loop out of clear fishing line and glue the two ends to the back of Santa's head.

Horseshoe Crab Santa

Equipment: 1 Horseshoe Crab
Paint (red, black, white,
. and flesh color)
Red ribbon
Cotton
Glue and craft spray

First, paint the face area with two coats of flesh color. Once dry, paint the hair and whiskers with two coats of white. The mouth is the natural line of the hinge that joins the two parts of the crab. Paint this red. Now paint the sensory spots of the crab black for the eyes, and then add white for the eyebrows.

Once dry, apply craft spray. Take a wide piece of red ribbon (about 6″ long, depending upon the size of the crab) and fold it as indicated in the photograph. Once stapled in the rear, it becomes Santa's hat. Place the ribbon on top of Santa's head and glue into place, both in front and in back. You may need to apply some pressure to hold the ribbon in place until the glue dries. Finally, add some cotton trim on top of the brim of the hat.

A large paper clip makes an ideal hanger when hooked into the ribbon at the back of Santa's head. The finished product may be hung on the wall, the door, or the tree.

Shell Night Light

Equipment:
    1 large Scallop shell
    1 Guide Light (See photograph. A
        Guide Light is entirely encased in
        plastic.)
    Glue and craft spray

Spray a brightly colored Scallop shell and let it dry. Take a Guide Light and glue the back of the shell onto it, using an excess of epoxy glue. Let dry, plug in, and you have a nice Sanibel shell night light.

116